SUSSEX SCENES

West Itchenor

SUSSEX SCENES

by MICHAEL H. C. BAKER

with drawings by the author

ROBERT HALE LIMITED · LONDON

© *Michael H. C. Baker 1978*
First published in Great Britain 1978

ISBN 0 7091 6997 3

Robert Hale Limited
Clerkenwell House
Clerkenwell Green
London EC1R 0HT

PHOTOSET AND PRINTED
IN GREAT BRITAIN BY
REDWOOD BURN LIMITED
TROWBRIDGE, BOUND BY
KEMP HALL BINDERY, OXFORD

Contents

COMPANION VOLUMES

Heart of England by Louise Wright and James Priddey
Rural Kent by John Boyle and John Berbier
Cotswold Heritage by Louise Wright and James Priddey

Illustrations

To my mother—and to Newhaven

CHAPTER ONE

Introduction

Some roads, most roads, get one from A to B, efficiently and safely, but with hardly more feeling, excitement or *élan* than a pipeline. But others are quite different; to spell out their name is to conjure up memories of great events, of visual delights, and brings on a tingle of anticipation. Such is the Brighton Road. It is not very old, no older than Brighton itself; but since Dr Russell and the Prince Regent transformed the latter from a fishing village into a resort without rival, most of the prominent men and women of the nation have travelled it. It is a testing ground and race-track for athletes, charity walkers, Edwardian ladies balancing on large balls, bath-tubs on wheels, ancient vehicles of every description, and above all has given a dozen or more generations of Londoners their first experience of Sussex. For them the fields and downs seen from the road or railway on their journey to the sea have become their definition of the countryside, just as Brighton is "the seaside", and if they go further afield they

judge what they see against Sussex. I was born and brought up mostly in South London, and have lived beside the sea and on the edge of the countryside in Sussex and in many other places, but Sussex will always be the yardstick by which I instinctively judge all else.

When I was a small boy in the years immediately after the Second World War, with petrol once again available to the private motorist and the coach operator, my father and I, like many others, would entertain ourselves for hours on a Sunday beside the Brighton Road counting the Austin Sevens and Morris Eights, the grey–green coaches of George Ewer and the orange luxury ones from Brixton, motor-cycle combinations, cars with spare wheels on the back, cars with spare wheels on the running board, Armstrong-Siddeleys, Sunbeam-Talbots, British Salmsons, Jowetts, the variety was endless. A couple of years earlier military convoys had been a common sight; they provoked rumours that "something was up", and one would be hurried away from shops which had large plate-glass windows, for fear they might shatter if there should be an air-raid. A few months after the war ended three ex-servicemen took over an ironmonger's shop near us on the Brighton Road and whenever I went past I would peer inside to get a glimpse of the heroic figures in charge. The fact that they wore grey warehouse coats and looked like every ironmonger I had ever seen did nothing to dim my visions of them piloting Lancasters over Berlin or

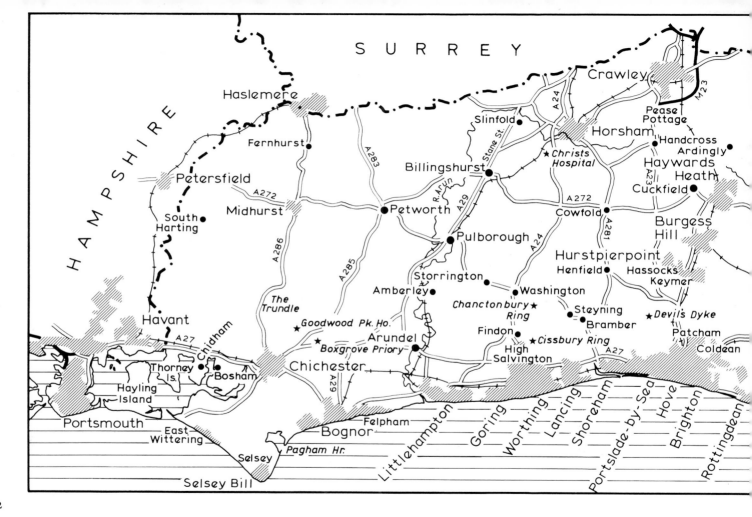

SURREY

Crawley

Haslemere

Slinfold

Pease
Pottage

M 23

Fernhurst

Horsham

A 24

Handcross
Ardingly

Stane St.

HAMPSHIRE

A 283

Billingshurst

★ Christs
Hospital

HAYWARDS
Heath

Petersfield

A 272

R. Arun

A 23

Midhurst

Petworth

A 29

Cowfold

Cuckfield

South
Harting

A 286

A 272

A 281

BURGESS
Hill

A 285

Pulborough

A 24

Hurstpierpoint

Henfield

Hassocks
Keymer

The
Trundle

Storrington

Washington

Amberley

Chanctonbury ★
Ring

Steyning

★ Devil's Dyke

Havant

Goodwood Pk. Ho.
★

Findon

Bramber

Patcham

Chidham

A 27

Arundel

High
Salvington

★ Cissbury Ring

Coldean

★ Boxgrove Priory

Thorney
Is.

Bosham

Chichester

A 29

A 27

Hayling
Island

Felpham

Littlehampton

Goring

Worthing

Lancing

Shoreham

Portslade-by-Sea

Hove

Brighton

Rottingdean

Portsmouth

East
Wittering

Bognor

Selsey

Pagham Hr.

Selsey Bill

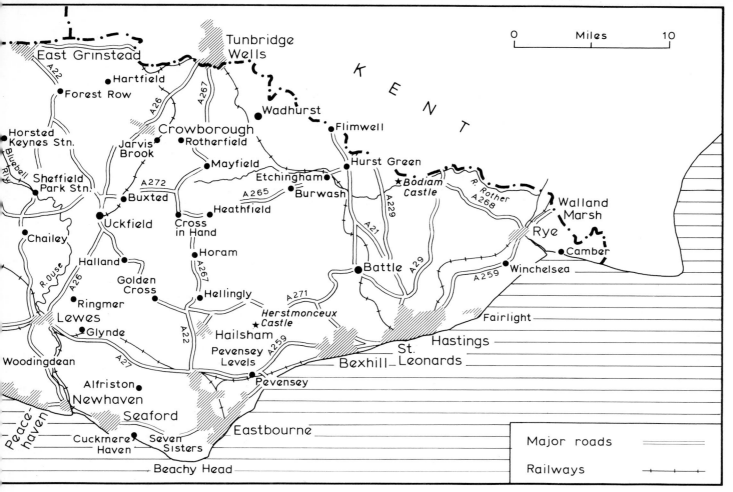

13

charging across the North African desert in a Sherman tank.

Later, when I was an art student, we would hitch-hike down to Brighton from where the country begins, at Coulsdon, and congregate under the Palace Pier to sketch the elderly day-trippers with their braces and rolled-up trousers and skirts tucked into the elastic of their bloomers; or else we would draw the pier itself, all encrusted iron-work and shabby glitter.

One of my many vacation jobs was to drive a lorry up and down the Brighton Road and elsewhere in Sussex. I soon had a good many of my illusions concerning the romantic nature of this particular occupation removed.

Perhaps the hardest assignment was to drive over to the gypsum works at Mountfield well before dawn and man-ually haul aboard 140-hundredweight sacks of plaster. A steam-engine would come wheezing down, enveloped in smoke and steam, from the works to the sidings, with the wagons containing the plaster, and one would then have to lift each sack on to the lorry. The first seventy were not so bad, but the second seventy had to be lifted on top of them, and by the time the last was in place, usually as dawn was forming silhouettes of the trees, one felt one had done a good day's work. Unloading the plaster in a builder's yard was relatively painless, but a factory or housing estate under construction, at Crawley for example, could be wretched, the ground often ankle deep in mud, the damp bottoms of the sacks always liable to burst open. The plaster got under one's fingernails, into one's hair, set one's teeth on edge and was altogether the nastiest commodity I had to carry. A more agreeable one was roofing-felt, which I had to collect from a factory in North London and then deliver the next day to merchants all over West Sussex, starting at Chichester, working my way along the coast through Bognor and Worthing, and ending up at Burgess Hill.

The most interesting of my regular journeys was to the London Docks to collect sisal for the rope-making factory at Hailsham. Nowadays man-made fibres have largely taken over, but ten years ago the factory required several lorry loads of sisal each week. Sometimes this would be collected from a warehouse in the now defunct Surrey Docks, but more often I would drive under the Thames by way of the Rotherhithe Tunnel on to the Isle of Dogs and into the heart of Dockland where the sisal would be hoisted out of a barge and onto my lorry. My last load before leaving the firm was the week's rubbish from Battle Rural District Council which I took up to a plant in South London.

The firm was a family one and from the life-style of the owners it was obvious that no one was making his fortune. Even so the wages of the drivers, which were comparable with those paid by other firms, were low, and to make a decent sort of living it was necessary to work overtime, often well beyond the legal maximum. Having previously

A restored carriage and pair, still in regular use, near Magham Down

worked for British Rail at Gatwick Airport and Victoria Station, it struck me forcibly that if the railways flouted regulations, both in regard to equipment and terms of employment, as much as the road haulage firms did, then the advantages which road transport has over rail would be greatly diminished.

Strictly speaking there is not one Brighton road, but rather a series of routes linking London and Brighton, which are constantly subject to alteration. The latest is the M23 motorway running from Merstham, at the southern end of the North Downs, to Peas Pottage, south of Crawley. It is an excellent road, which by-passes the A23 bottlenecks at Redhill and around Crawley, and cannot be said to have disfigured the countryside, except perhaps where it has cut a swathe through St Leonards Forest and veered too near the parish church of Worth. This latter is one of the outstanding pieces of architecture in the county, indeed there are few more comprehensive Saxon remains in Britain, and although trees hide it from the motorway they cannot prevent the constant rumble of the traffic intruding where there was formerly silence.

The A23 is not much of a road in Surrey, but once across the Sussex border it improves considerably, being largely dual carriageway from Gatwick onwards. It originally ran right across what is now the main runway of the airport, and was diverted to the east alongside the railway when the old aerodrome was transformed into London's second airport after the Second World War. The Southern Railway had built a station to serve the aerodrome in the 1930s all concrete, curved glass and metal window frames—south of the original racecourse station; it was not until the 1950s that this latter became the present, much modernized, Gatwick Airport. When our school was taken to an air display at Gatwick in 1949 the racecourse was closed but still intact and the aerodrome was nothing but a large grass field. The original control tower remains, as does the first hangar and part of the field, now used by helicopters. The aerodrome station, however, is derelict, and the old racecourse station has been transformed into an integral part of the airport buildings. Electric trains depart for London every ten minutes or so during the day and hourly through the night. The A23 passes right under the terminal buildings, avoiding the luggage and the air hostesses, and there is a direct link to the M23, one mile to the east. No airport in the country can match Gatwick's communications.

Immediately beyond Gatwick is Crawley, which the A23 avoids by way of a tree-lined dual carriageway looping around to the west of the town centre. When, in the late 1920s, weekend motoring ceased to be just a pastime of the rich and became something more widely indulged in, the Brighton Road was almost the first to suffer and Crawley was one of the earliest towns to be inflicted with traffic-jams. The result was the first by-pass in Sussex,

Gatwick Airport

although it was not completed until after the Second World War. From the last of the numerous roundabouts in the vicinity of Crawley, the A23 climbs up to the junction with the M23 at Peas Pottage and then sweeps down through the trees of St Leonards Forest into its most attractive stretch, the two gently curving carriageways, often some distance apart and at different levels, until they merge on the level beyond Bolney with the South Downs extending across the horizon some five miles distant. South of Bolney, to the east, the Keymer–Hassocks–Hurstpierpoint conglomeration stretches out, without quite reaching the A23; alongside the road on the western side is the All-England Jumping Course at Hickstead.

Hickstead is owned by Douglas Bunn, a Sussex man born at Selsey in 1928, a barrister and a one-time member of the English jumping team. During the 1950s he became increasingly aware of the need to set up a permanent course which would enable English riders to get on equal terms with those from the Continent. When Hickstead Place came on the market in 1959, the first time for over 400 years, Bunn realized that its position beside the A23, and only one hour's drive from London, was ideal, and he opened what many considered to be the presumptuously titled All-England Jumping Course in May 1960. For a time it seemed as if Bunn's critics might be right, but gradually the thirty-acre course came into its own and for some years now it has been considered the leading one in the country, attracting the best riders from all over the world and great crowds to watch them.

A more controversial pursuit popular with the horse-owning fraternity in Sussex is hunting. It is perhaps unfortunate that my most memorable encounter with a fox-hunting person was in a village post-office with a lady who so closely resembled the broad-beamed, red-faced, tweed-suited traditional caricature that I at first suspected she had escaped from a W.I. pageant. She was exulting over the treatment of a group of anti-bloodsports campaigners who had been beaten up at a recent show with such ferocity that the usually neutral local paper had been provoked into protest on their behalf. On the other hand anyone who has read Siegfried Sassoon's *Memoirs of a Fox-Hunting Man*, much of which is set in East Sussex, cannot but be aware that it is quite possible both to enthuse over riding over other people's property and at the same time be perfectly kindly and considerate in most other respects. As to the keeping down of foxes, most farmers today consider shooting the most effective method.

Whatever one thinks of fox-hunting—and ever since coming across the remains of a fox strewn across two fields as a child I have not liked it—there is surely little to be said in favour of otter-hunting. The first hunt in Sussex was established in 1903. A description by one of those taking part in an otter-hunt in the Withyham district twenty years later more vividly illustrates the pointless brutality of the practice than any intended condemnation. After remarking that Sussex is "a very lovely county and in parts resembles Devonshire . . . with the added attraction of not being so far from Town, which enables one to reach a meet of the hounds easily in the morning and to be home for dinner in the evening", the piece ends thus: "the otter eventually begins to tire . . . then it is that hounds show their mettle and knowledge as they give him no peace, until one hound gets a hold, and the rest of the pack joining him, they kill their otter in mid-stream".

Although otters eat fish, they hardly kill enough to affect the overall numbers—and who is to say they do not have as much right to them as any human fisherman—they also eat water-voles, moorhens, frogs, ducks and rabbits. In the last ten years their numbers have declined dramatically and Britain is the only European country which provides no protection for the otter. Surveys carried out by the Mammal Society and the Nature Conservancy Council are a good deal more thorough than data supplied by otter-hunters, so the latter cannot justify their activities on this count; and unless hunting is brought quickly to an end schemes to set up otter havens in various parts of the country, including the Sussex rivers where otters were once so common, will be too late.

We seemed to have strayed a good way from the Brighton Road so let us get back, to the Downs, to the famous Clayton windmills, Jack and Jill, and the traffic-jams which can begin where the A23 merges with the A281 Horsham road, or at Pyecombe where the A273 comes in from Haywards Heath and also from London. Pyecombe, where Sussex crooks are still forged, is two miles north of the Cenotaph-like stone pillars which mark the Brighton boundary at Patcham. The sea is still the best part of four miles away and the A23 continues across the Brighton ring road which climbs steeply out of the valley, eastwards towards the Lewes road and Sussex University, westwards through a ludicrously narrow arch in the direction of Hove. The A23 follows the course of a stream which rises at Patcham, past a handsome park with flower beds ingeniously arranged to form patterns and designs, which used to belong to the manor of Preston, although both Preston and Patcham villages have long since lost their independence and become suburbs of Brighton. Nevertheless, it is grass and trees practically all the way once the magnificent curved viaduct and the shopping area around the junction of the Lewes and London roads have been negotiated. Beyond is the Steine, around which Brighton has grown, with the Royal Pavilion beside it, and here the Brighton Road ends, for we can go no further save to walk to the end of the Palace Pier.

Brighton is by far the largest town in the county but it is not its administrative centre; the county town of East Sussex being Lewes and of West Sussex, Chichester. Both

The veteran commercial vehicle run to Brighton on the A23 at Handcross

are ancient towns, which existed when Dr Russell, the Prince Regent and the great resort they were to bring into existence lay far in the future, along with the notion that anyone should enter salt water of his own volition. There are those who regret the passing of the Sussex which existed in those days, when only fishermen, boat-builders, sailors, smugglers, flora and fauna were to be found on the sea-shore. Whether the county is now "spoilt", as some would claim, the visitor must decide for himself. There is probably no more popular county in all England than Sussex. It is close to London, no part of it being much more than ninety minutes travelling time by car or train from the West End; and having been in the business of catering for the holidaymaker longer than anywhere else it has no prejudice against strangers, any that it might once have possessed being effectively stifled in the interests of commerce. The Industrial Revolution brought about the end of the ancient Sussex iron industry but the prosperity of the county barely faltered for it was able to entice both the new working class and its masters to its blossoming seaside resorts. It thus reaped the benefits of the industrial age, whilst largely escaping, except in Brighton, having to pay the price of bad housing, dirt and disease, which were common in the industrial centres themselves.

It would be idle to pretend that every development along the seventy-seven miles of coastline has been of un-alloyed aesthetic delight; one is grateful that the strenuous efforts of preservationists in the 1930s ensured the peace of Cuckmere Haven and that the passing of large areas of the Downs around Beachy Head and Birling Gap into the safe hands of the National Trust means they will never be built upon. Peacehaven, despite producing a Miss United Kingdom, is not beautiful; neither are the caravan-sites of the Selsey Peninsula. At the same time, however, the exploitation of Sussex resulted in the transformation of Brighthelmston into the incomparable Brighton; and the reader might also consider the delight brought to millions upon millions of children by the sands of Bognor; the tranquillity to generations of old people by the ordered serenity of Eastbourne and Bexhill; the glory, touching even the most inartistic soul, of an autumn sunset behind Worthing Pier; and the accumulated excitement of all the families down the years who have ever set off for a day at the seaside since the first train pulled out of London Bridge for Brighton on 21st September 1841.

Sussex is middle class and prosperous. Because it almost completely escaped industrialization in the nineteenth century it has no great organized working class outside Brighton. There the Trades Council was founded in 1890 and since then has ensured socialist representation on the town council; indeed for a period in the 1960s the Kemp Town division returned a Labour M.P. In the 1905 general election a Liberal was returned for Brighton and a year later when there was a countrywide Liberal landslide two

21

Playing bowls at Bognor

members of that party represented the town. Otherwise, like most rural and seaside areas, Sussex has been and is solidly Conservative.

Administratively the county is divided into West and East, the dividing line skirting the eastern and southern perimeters of Crawley and then running due south, parallel with and to the west of the A23, reaching the sea at Portslade. Since April 1974 there have been seven local authorities in East Sussex, Hove, Brighton, Eastbourne, Hastings, Lewes, Wealden and Rother. Their combined population in 1971 was 747,974.

The less populous West Sussex, with 492,495 inhabitants, also possesses seven district councils. These are Adur, Arun, Chichester, Crawley, Horsham, Mid-Sussex and Worthing.

Hundreds of parish councils still exist and although their powers are very limited they give those that care about such things the feeling that they have a say in the affairs of the community. Almost every village in Sussex has its cricket green and for 250 years the county has been a stronghold of the game. Soccer, needing an industrial, working class base, has seldom flourished at the highest level in rural or seaside areas and in Sussex only Brighton and Hove Albion has achieved Football League status. Founded in 1902, the club has mostly been in the third division, although it is presently in the second. For a short while the mercurial Brian Clough was its manager and brought the club its greatest fame, if not success.

The Brighton Urban Structure Plan of 1970 noted that fishing was "a major growth sport", from beach, boat and pier; on August Bank Holiday, 1970, the staggering total of 560 fishing- and pleasure-boats of various sorts was recorded within two miles of Brighton beach. Taking part that day in the most popular seaside recreation of all—sitting on the beach—were an estimated 40,000 people. The beaches were, the report concludes, "well-used but at only 50 per cent of what is judged to be a comfortable capacity".

Of the county's total population of approximately $1\frac{1}{4}$ million, one half lives in the nine principal resorts, one third lives in the area bounded by Lancing in the west and Seaford in the east. Brighton has 161,351 inhabitants; Worthing 88,000; Hove 73,000; Hastings 72,000; Eastbourne 71,000; Bognor 34,000; Bexhill 33,000; Littlehampton 18,000; and Seaford 16,000. If we add the two ports of Newhaven and Shoreham, the largely residential areas of Portslade-by-Sea and Southwick, the villages of the Selsey Peninsula, the small town of Selsey itself, the former ports of Pevensey, Winchelsea and Rye, and other settlements along the coast, we see how great is the pull of the seaside.

The great counterbalance is Crawley. Designated a new town after the Second World War, it has grown sevenfold since then and now has a population in excess of

70,000 and still rising. It has a labour force of 33,000 greater than any other town in Sussex apart from Brighton. Further south, in the heart of the county, are Haywards Heath and Burgess Hill. Places of no significance until the coming of the railway, they were not very large even thirty years ago; although Haywards Heath, being a junction, had grown sufficiently to eclipse its once important neighbour, Cuckfield. Since the Second World War Haywards Heath and Burgess Hill have grown until their combined population is now around 40,000. The Strategic Plan for the South-East, commissioned by the Government in 1968 and published in 1970, envisages their continued growth to the extent that they will meet around the turn of the century. Unwelcome though this might be, sensible planning is clearly vital. In the 1920s and early '30s there was very little and we are living with the consequences. In that part of the county nearest London—the northern forest slopes—ribbons of houses stretched deep into the countryside from Crowborough, East Grinstead, Three Bridges and Horsham. Many, in a period when land was relatively cheap, were palatial, especially around Crowborough and Jarvis Brook. In 1935 the much-needed Restriction of Ribbon Development Act was passed, which initially forbade the construction, without the consent of the highway authority, of houses on roads debouching on a by-pass, or within 220 yards of the middle of a by-pass. In East Sussex it was soon extended to include all classified roads, and in West Sussex to 120 stretches of varying lengths; and this effectively put an end to ribbon development.

Until the 1974 local government revisions Gatwick Airport was in Surrey, but it is now in West Sussex. It has always looked to Crawley and further south for most of its workforce, which at present numbers 16,000. In an area where unemployment has always been much lower than the national average it could not be argued that any expansion is needed to provide jobs. Pressure for its expansion would disappear if a third London airport were to be built but this will surely not happen now, and it may be that the Channel Tunnel would have proved the least of all the possible evils, if evil it be.

Burgess Hill and Haywards Heath might almost be considered suburbia, so great is the percentage of their working population which travels to Brighton, Crawley, Gatwick, Croydon and London. Indeed more season ticket holders travel up from Haywards Heath to London than from any other station in the county, Brighton having been ousted from this position in the mid 1960s. At the other extreme there were thirteen commuters from East Worthing and fourteen from Pevensey and Westham at the last count. However, the grand total runs into many thousands and there is no station with a direct service to London anywhere in the county which does not send up its daily contingent.

Great Ouse Viaduct

25

Ploughing with horses in the Weald in the 1930s

At the same time it is easy to over-emphasize the influence of London upon Sussex life. To those who can afford to travel to and from the capital each working day it looms large in their lives; for the great majority it is far enough away to play little part. They make the occasional

sight-seeing or shopping trip, as they would if they lived 200 miles away, but that is all.

It is a point worth remembering for it is all too easy when travelling to the coast by car or train to imagine that Sussex sees itself as little more than the playground for Londoners. For a lot of people their lives are still very much centred upon the area immediately around their homes, and this is as true of teenagers and young married couples as it is of the middle-aged and elderly. Superficially Sussex may seem to be totally changed since the days before the Prince Regent, the railway and the motor car. Package tours may take off from Gatwick for the Costa Brava every few minutes at the height of the tourist season and the whole county is apparently awheel at bank holidays; but people still raise families, earn their livings and do their business in one place. The great mass of the population go about their lives, whether in the suburbs of a resort, in an inland town, or in a village, largely oblivious to and unobserved by the visitor.

For all that the seaside dominates the county, elsewhere, despite the growth of the inland towns, Sussex is still essentially rural. The countryside unfolds before the traveller approaching from the north in three succeeding and distinct regions. First there are the forest slopes, encountered immediately beyond the Surrey border. Almost all of Sussex has its richly wooded areas, but the principal remains of the great forest which once covered it are

Haycutting near Hailsham today

27

Threshing under the Downs near Ringmer in 1945

28

found in the north. The best views of them are to be had either from the train travelling between Three Bridges and Balcombe, the railway cutting through the heart of the Tilgate Forest and eventually tunnelling under it; or immediately south of Forest Row on the A22. This latter winds its way down from East Grinstead to the valley of the infant Medway, a river generally associated with Kent but which rises not far from Forest Row and forms the Kent-Sussex boundary for some miles. From here it climbs deep into the forest, past signs warning the motorist to beware of deer (which certainly exist but which very seldom venture within sight of the main roads), on beyond Broadstone Warren, a 400-acre camping site used by Boy Scouts from all over the country, to the summit at Wych Cross where the Lewes road diverges. Here the forest takes on a different aspect, the dense oak and beech woods giving way to gorse covered heathland with extensive views in all directions—to the North and South Downs, eastwards beyond Crowborough Beacon (the highest point of the Ashdown Forest), into Kent, and westwards to the Worth, Tilgate and St Leonards Forests.

Beyond is the heart of the Weald, undulating country with abundant woodlands, originally occupying an area of roughly 4,000 square miles, extending over the borders of Sussex into Kent, Surrey and Hampshire. Daniel Defoe, in his *Tour Thro the Whole Island of Great Britain*, describes a journey through the Weald from "Tun-bridge" to Lewes, and writes that he came "through the deepest, dirtiest but in many ways the richest and most profitable country in all that part of England". Surfacing of the roads has largely removed the dirt but it is still rich farming land, an area of picturesque villages and small towns, once part of the great forest of Andredsweald but increasingly under cultivation since the latter days of the Iron Age.

The history of Sussex begins on the South Downs where the relics of its earliest inhabitants have been found in Neolithic camps at Whitehawk by Brighton Racecourse, at the Trundle north of Chichester, at Cissbury above Worthing, and elsewhere.

Part of an escarpment 180 miles long which extends, as the North Downs, from the cliffs of Dover through Kent and Surrey into Hampshire and then swings around Petersfield, the South Downs proper begin just inside Hampshire and continue westwards behind Chichester and Arundel until they reach the sea at Brighton. Thence they form a magnificent series of cliffs, culminating in the 536 foot-high Beachy Head above Eastbourne.

Beyond the Downs is the sea. Between Brighton and Eastbourne it breaks against their foot; in the west it is seen as a shimmering, blue-grey haze between the Selsey Peninsula and the Isle of Wight; whilst to the east the coastline continues for the best part of thirty miles from Beachy Head, around the Pevensey Marshes, past the cliffs of

Hastings and Fairlight to the Romney Marshes. Solitude is not as instantly obtainable as it is up on the Downs, but nevertheless it is easily enough found by those who care to look. There are many occasions when even the beach beside the Palace Pier at Brighton is deserted and there are always stretches of the coastline, in Chichester Harbour, around Cuckmere Haven and near Rye, where even on the sunniest bank holiday the day-trippers seldom penetrate.

Nevertheless the Sussex coast is essentially for people.

Not all of it is more beautiful as a consequence, although there is some superb seaside architecture, but so rich is the variety in the seventy or so miles between Selsey and Camber, the grandeur and vulgarity of Brighton, the gentility of Eastbourne and Bexhill, the antiquity of Hastings, the booming commerce at Newhaven, the unconsummated aspirations of Bognor and Seaford, and the unassailable superiority of Hove, that the gain is far greater than the loss.

View westwards from the Devil's Dyke

CHAPTER TWO

Rye to Battle

Rye was a town when the *Domesday Book* was compiled and a little over 100 years later became, with Winchelsea, one of the Cinque Ports. It stands on a hill and still has the wooded slopes around Peasmarsh and Udimore to the north. But to the south all is changed, for where once was the open sea, land extends for two miles and Rye remains a port only by virtue of the River Rother. This is deep enough to allow timber ships from Scandinavia and Russia to sail up to the wharf at the south-eastern edge of the town, but they can go no further; although a lock, overlooked by a windmill, enables small pleasure craft to penetrate further into the Levels behind Rye. From here on and up past Bodiam the Rother forms the boundary between Kent and Sussex. At Rye the Rother joins the Brede and the Tillingham by the fishmarket and close to the Rother Ironworks and flows on past Rye Harbour to the sea.

Rye Harbour is a quite separate entity, a place in its own right, the result of an attempt made at the end of the Tudor era—when it was realized that the original port's great days were over—to revive the town's sea-faring traditions. It was constructed at what was then the mouth of the estuary. Today it is a nondescript collection of cement and gravel works, a village church, a bus yard, a few houses, a pub called the William the Conqueror, some converted railway carriages and a yacht centre. The sea continued to recede and for a good many years Rye Harbour, like the original port of Rye, has had to make do with the river.

Although not easy to picture today, except perhaps down by the harbour, Rye was at one period a centre of industry. In the mid-seventeenth century the Huguenots, fleeing persecution in France, arrived in England. They were by tradition weavers and a great many came to Sussex, settled and added a further strain to the native craft. A crude form of weaving had long been practised in Kent and East Sussex, but until the middle of the fourteenth century the lords and ladies who wanted something more decorative than the natural shades and coarse weaves of the native product had to buy from abroad. Edward III seems to have been the first English king to have done anything about this when he imported skilled weavers from the Low Countries. They had always used English wool and soon settled in Kent and Sussex, in time passing their skills on to the local people. Rye particularly appealed

Rye, from the river-bank

Rye, a view southwards from the town walls

to the Huguenots. Large numbers made their first sanctuary in the town and, finding it an agreeable place, well used to French ways through centuries of trade and wars, stayed. There was a period when one in seven of the population was a Huguenot, and a village north-west of the town where many of them lived is to this day called Rye Foreign.

The weaving industry in Sussex eventually went the same way as Wealden iron, killed off by the substitution of coal for charcoal as a fuel and also by competition from the more highly mechanized mills of Scotland; but the Huguenot weavers are still remembered, for there has been so much intermarriage in the three succeeding centuries that there can be few long established families living between the Pevensey and Romney marshes which do not contain some French blood—always supposing they had not previously absorbed some of the Norman variety. Anglicized versions of French names, Pont and Vidler for example, are common.

Almost all of Rye's buildings, packed tightly together beside the hilly, cobbled streets and dominated by the squat tower of the parish church of St Mary, are of architectural and historic interest, and the town has long been popular with artists and writers. Many of England's kings and queens have stayed in Rye, often on their way to or from France, and its relationship with that country has shaped its development. In medieval times it suffered a succession of raids, once losing the bells of its parish church, although they were recovered two days later; and as a leading member of the Cinque Ports it gave the French as good as it got. Goodness knows how many smuggling stories—true or fiction—have been set in Rye, although the subject was not one which attracted the town's most famous writer, Henry James. Smuggling went on into the mid 1800s, a fact which John Wesley deplored on his visits during the latter part of the previous century; he preached his last outdoor sermon in the shade of an ash tree in Winchelsea churchyard on 7th October 1790. Rye maintained its ancient traditions of providing ships for the Royal Navy as late as the Crimean War, when it built some mortars; and pleasure and fishing vessels are still built in the town down in the yards beneath the ancient walls.

Whilst Kent is the traditional hop-growing county of south-east England, the district around Rye is sufficiently close to the border for the fields of pale green hops, climbing skywards like over-enthusiastic runner beans, to be a familiar sight. Not so long ago they grew in abundance in the Horham, Mayfield, Wartling and Uckfield areas, persisting in the latter as late as the 1930s. There was at one time an isolated hop farm at Bepton, near Midhurst, and whilst this was unusually far west, converted oast houses are common in the eastern part of the county.

The bottom floor of the oast house was the furnace, and

Oast house at Flimwell, within a few yards of the Kent border

above this the hops were spread on battens, often covered with horsehair. The heat passed through the hair, drying the hops, and the steam passed into the atmosphere through the cone, that most distinctive feature of an oast house. The drying process took upwards of twenty-four hours. Originally the hops were crushed by men wearing hob-nailed boots, a comically appropriate contrast to the bare feet employed by lesser nationalities when pressing their grapes. In the late nineteenth century the boots were replaced by hop-presses, but across the border in Kent mechanization and more efficient organization went much further than this and largely accounted for the dying out of the industry in all but the south-east corner of Sussex.

Through the Sussex hop-fields flows the Eastern Rother. Although Rye is the only town on its course it is a river with many industrial associations (albeit chiefly historical ones) the remains of which are now considered charming and picturesque. Two and a half miles north-east of Rye and within a mile of the Kent border is the Royal Military Canal. In the latter part of the eighteenth century and at the beginning of the nineteenth there was considerable enthusiasm in Sussex for canal building, or more accurately, the canalization of the rivers, and for a few years until the railway arrived a fair amount of water-borne traffic was carried about the county. But the Royal Military Canal was an exception and although built during this period had a quite different *raison d'être*, being part of the defences raised to repel Napoleon. It extended from Sandgate in the east to the Rother, and then from a junction with the Brede below Winchelsea to the sea at Cliff End, east of Fairlight. It was begun in 1807 and involved much labour, although William Cobbett, 16 years later, tartly remarked upon its chances of keeping out an army "which has so often crossed the Rhine and the Danube".

The canal was to provide a line of defence to protect the Weald beyond, and it was amongst this wooded border country that the iron industry flourished for a thousand years and more. Ernest Straker's standard work on the subject, *Wealden Iron*, records a great many ironworks in the area, and the last active one was at Ashburnham, near Battle, which ceased working in 1824. Few substantial relics of any of the sites remain, but if one stands by the bridge over the stream at Ashburnham one may look down into the water which even now flows a deep red. Quite possibly some of the cottages beside the stream were once the homes of the ironworkers and a walk of a mile along a track will bring one to the site of the works where more cottages and other buildings once associated with the forge remain.

The Rother forms the boundary between Sussex and Kent for some seven miles from north of Iden to just before the great castle at Bodiam. For centuries the river

Bodiam Castle, with hopfields in front

was the principal means of communication between Rye and Winchelsea and the Weald, and the iron products came down it on their way to be exported all over the world. Bodiam stood guard over the Rother, having been built principally to deter the French. From the fifteenth to the nineteenth centuries the castle was allowed to decay but was preserved in its present ruined but impressive state, first by Baron Ashcombe of the Cubitt engineering family and then by Lord Curzon. It passed to the National Trust on the latter's death in 1926.

Alongside the Rother runs the Kent and East Sussex Railway, a line operated by enthusiasts with a collection of vintage carriages and steam locomotives, including one from Norway. It was founded in the early years of the present century by Lieutenant-Colonel Holman Fred Stephens, son of the Pre-Raphaelite painter and an archetypal Victorian; resourceful, inventive, authoritarian and a trifle eccentric. Stephens, a true believer in lost causes, made it his mission in life to build, own and operate rural branch lines in parts of the country where the big companies could see no prospect of profit—justifiably in most cases. He built three lines in Sussex, two of which, the Rye and Camber and the Hundred of Mahood and Selsey, have vanished leaving little trace; but the Kent and East Sussex, also known as the Rother Valley, was rather more successful, and in 1948 when it was absorbed by British Railways trains still ran over its entire length between Headcorn and Robertsbridge. Stephens' lines never made him or anyone else a fortune and even in their brief heyday only covered their costs by employing second, third and fourth hand carriages and locomotives and some pioneer, bone-shaking railbuses built from the discarded remains—in one case—of a London tram, and various other oddments no one else wanted. Stephens never married. He had a house at Robertsbridge and another at Tonbridge but he spent most of his life travelling about the country watching his trains run up and down Welsh mountains, along the clifftops of Somerset and elsewhere. When he visited the Kent and East Sussex he travelled in a special carriage built for Queen Victoria in the 1840s. He died in 1931, by which time his railways were already losing their battle against the motor. Hops kept the Kent and East Sussex going and during the picking season it carried thousands of East Enders and their friends in through trains to and from London. British Railways kept sections of the line open for goods traffic until the 1960s, by which time the preservation movement was getting into its stride and eventually after long legal wrangles, chiefly over the many level crossings, a short section was reopened in 1974. Put back into working order by enthusiasts, schoolchildren and youth groups, the railway has of late received Government aid enabling further expansion and it is set fair to become as great an attraction as the Bluebell.

Robertsbridge, the one-time terminus of the line, marks

the western limit of the hop-growing area. It is either a small town or large village, according to one's fancy, dating from the founding of a Cistercian abbey shortly after the Norman Conquest. A market was granted in 1225 and a yearly fair thirty years later but Robertsbridge has remained important only in the immediate locality, although the coming of the London to Hastings railway line in 1857 resulted in a certain amount of expansion which has continued in a modest way down to the present time. The A21 runs through the middle of Robertsbridge, which does not add to its otherwise quite considerable charms, and it badly needs a by-pass. The parish church is more than a mile away, in Salehurst, close to the remains of the Cistercian abbey which moved there from Robertsbridge in 1210. The remains are now part of a farmhouse.

Four miles south of Robertsbridge is Battle. There used to be a guide at the abbey—there may still be—who asked every school party the date of the battle. He would never accept 1066 but always insisted on the month and the day, which he seldom got. For the record, it was 14th October, Harold's birthday. Harold had been king for just over nine months, although he had been virtual ruler, under Edward the Confessor, for the best part of fourteen years. The abbey stands on the site of the battle. Much of it is now in ruins, albeit substantial ones, and the remainder is a boarding-school. The gateway is in the centre of the town,

Sheep grazing on the slopes where Harold fought William on 14th October, 1066. The ruins at Battle Abbey stand behind

in the market place. The view beyond it, down the grassy slope, is that which confronted Harold as he stood on the crest of the hill with his English army. How near he came to defeating the Norman invaders gathered on the marshy land at the bottom is known by every schoolboy; but it might be worth adding that not all historians support the generally held notion that their retreat was a ruse to lure Harold's men from the heights. It is possible that the flight was in earnest and that Harold, a bold leader, ordered his men to follow them. But there is no dispute over the outcome of the eight-hour battle.

Something like 16,000 men—fairly equally divided between the two armies—took part, and at the end of the day a large proportion was either dead or dying. The English nobility was decimated. Whatever Harold's shortcomings as a politician and tactician he was a brave fighter and years later when William had completed his conquest of England he returned to the site of the battle and had the abbey erected. On the spot where Harold fell was set the high altar. Perhaps inevitably there were stories that Harold had not been killed. There is a legend that the body taken to Waltham Abbey was not his, and that he lived on as a monk for many years. There is a German legend to this effect, and another recounts a supposed meeting between Henry I and Harold at Chester sometime in the period between 1101 and 1103; 'Harold was then very old and was believed to have died soon afterwards'. It is not surprising that there were those unable to accept so momentous an event, but most historians take the view that the last Anglo-Saxon king died on the slopes of Senlac Hill.

On the evening before the battle, William vowed he would build a monastery on the site and shortly after the Conquest it was begun. *La Bataille* was the name given to the place by William the day after the battle; the battlefield being called *Sanquelac* (Lake of Blood), which has now become Senlac. By the time the abbey was ready for consecration in 1095, William Rufus was on the throne, and he attended the ceremony, along with the Archbishop of Canterbury and most of the prominent secular and religious leaders of the time. The ordinary people were there too, in great numbers, some from the growing town of Battle, based on a Saxon settlement.

The abbey belonged to the Benedictines, an order founded in Rome in the sixth century. It was one especially concerned with the sick, and at Battle the monks had charge of a lepers' hospital; a wall by the Wellington Hotel is thought to be a remnant of it. When the abbey was dissolved in 1538 a thorough job was done, and apart from the valuables and the money gained from the sale of the fittings, all of which went to the Crown, much of the fabric was removed and sold or used as building materials. The monks of Battle seem not to have been corrupted by possessions and position, as had many others elsewhere; many, so it is said, went to live at Senlac House in the town, whilst the abbot retired to what is now the Abbot's Cottage.

Battle Abbey estate came up for sale in 1976 and there were fears that it might be sold piecemeal or to developers, but it was acquired for the nation and its future is secure.

Between Battle and Robertsbridge, to the east of the A21, is one of the county's principal modern industrial sites. In the mid-1870s members of the British Association

The gypsum works at Mountfield

sunk a bore hole at Mountfield in order to investigate the rock formation, and quite by accident came across a rich seam of gypsum. Gypsum is an essential component of cement and plaster and for 100 years it has been mined on a large scale at Mountfield. The mines lie in a valley screened by the lie of the land and by thick woods, so their presence is scarcely noticed. They are nevertheless extensive and supply much of the building trade in Sussex and the South-East. The main shaft is 160 feet deep and in some ways the workings resemble a coal-mine. They are, however, safe, there being no danger from gas, and naked lights may be used. On being brought to the surface the gypsum is burnt in kilns, taken to crushing mills, ground, sifted and bagged. During the winter months, from early in the morning, long before dawn, lorries arrive at Mountfield to load up and then go trundling off, either along the A21 to London or south through Battle to the coast. The works have their own private railway, connected to the London to Hastings line, and wagons of cement and plaster are brought down from the mines to the loading bays. An average sized lorry load is eight tons, broken down into 160 sacks, and each sack has to be unloaded by the driver when it reaches its destination, which may be a building site, a yard or a wholesalers. In a year a driver deals with tens of thousands of sacks, often in wet, dirty conditions.

Another product essential to the building trade is lime, and there are numerous downland quarries in Sussex which provide it, Lewes being the centre of the industry.

Close by Mountfield is Darwell Reservoir, the second largest inland expanse of water in the county, the largest being Weir Wood Reservoir south of East Grinstead. The third largest and the most recently completed is the Arlington Reservoir, beneath the Downs and close to the Long Man of Wilmington. I once met an Irishman painting the railings around it whose previous job had been as a footman at Buckingham Palace; he had left because the wages were not good enough.

The Rother, a tributary of which feeds the Darwell reservoir, flows north-westwards from Robertsbridge through the village of Etchingham, past fields which frequently flood and where adders are to be found, and on towards its source near Rotherfield, the origins of which go back to the eighth century. Rotherfield stands 500 feet above sea-level and close by Argos Hill, from the slopes of which flow streams which feed the Rother, the Ouse and the Medway. Argos Hill is one of my favourite spots in Sussex. It attracts few visitors and yet there is scarcely a finer vantage point in all of south-east England. To the east the wooded ridges and sloping fields, dotted with farmhouses, the Victorian roofline of Mayfield School and the spire of Wadhurst church, stretch into Kent; to the south beyond the undulating chimneys and roofs of Mayfield, where the Archbishops of Canterbury once

Rotherfield

Mayfield and the Weald from Argos Hill

44

lived, there are more tree-covered slopes and the bare
South Downs in the far distance; whilst to the west the
unbroken forests of Ashdown and St Leonards stretch for
twenty miles. To the north, on the summit of the hill,
stands a handsome windmill. A post-mill, it is in excellent
condition after restoration and was one of the last working ones in the country, having remained in use until 1927.
At that time there were some fifty post-mills still active in
Sussex; 100 years earlier there had been four times as
many. By the beginning of the Second World War, of the
ninety in existence only a handful were in use, and many
were in various states of dereliction. The only active post-
mill was at Cross-in-Hand, whilst the tower-mills at
Stonecross and Polegate were virtually the only ones still
in occasional use for grinding.

Mills were often destroyed by fire, usually caused by
sparks from the stones left turning by an inattentive miller
after all the grain had passed through. The famous one at
Rye burnt down in 1930 but a clause in the tenancy of the
adjoining bakery stipulated that it had to be maintained
and so it was rebuilt as a dummy. By this time interest in
windmills was being aroused and Arthur Foord Hughes
held an exhibition in a Bond Street gallery of paintings of
every Sussex windmill then in existence. Hughes, who
lived in Hastings and was co-author of a book on Sussex
mills, was more widely known in the guise of Tom
Brown, for his father had been the original illustrator of

The mill at Argos Hill

45

the book and had used his son as a model for the hero; as a baby Arthur Hughes had also been painted by Rossetti, who lived for a time in Hastings and married Elizabeth Siddal at St Clements in that town.

The *Domesday Book* mentions approximately 150 mills in Sussex, but these would all have been water-powered, the windmill probably being introduced in medieval times by returning crusaders who had come across them in the lands around the eastern Mediterranean. The oldest record of one is at Bishopstone in 1199. The first were owned by the lords of the manor, later by villeins. The miller was one of the most important members of the community and a key figure in its prosperity.

Some mills, at Barnham for example, remained in business using electric power after the sweeps had ceased to turn. The revival of interest in the windmill and milling in the 1930s promoted the preservation movement, one of its first successes being the smock mill at Shipley which Hilaire Belloc owned for nearly fifty years until his death in 1953. Another famous mill is that at Punnetts Town which has been in the possession of the same milling family for nearly 200 years. Today none remains in commercial use in the county, but dedicated work and careful research is ensuring the restoration of many to working order.

CHAPTER THREE

Crowborough to Crawley

Until the railway arrived in 1881 Crowborough was a small village high on the southern slopes of the Ashdown Forest, close to the Kent border; Tunbridge Wells, eight miles to the north-east, represented the outside world. London could only be reached indirectly, either by way of Tunbridge Wells or by a series of tracks and lanes leading eventually to the old Roman road through Edenbridge or to East Grinstead. Even when the railway arrived it was only a branch line and the trains were slow and not very frequent, but there were sufficient to bring speculators and estate agents the forty miles from the capital to the breezy heights which culminate in the 800-foot-high Crowborough Beacon. They went home and composed paeans in praise of the health-giving properties of the fresh air, the pines, and the peace, and soon grand villas were springing up all the way up the hill from the village to the beacon. Large slices of land, much of it within the perimeter of the Ashdown Forest, were bought up, and although as late as 1939 the entire population was only around the 2,000 mark, the ribbon development all around Crowborough Cross, the centre of what was now a town, was extensive.

A great many successful people from London owned property in the district, the most famous being Sir Arthur Conan Doyle, and there were faltering attempts to establish a spa of sorts on the heights. Perhaps there were visions of creating a rival to Tunbridge Wells. Certainly the setting was superb, and one of the hotels claimed to be "a wee bit of Scotland in Sussex", a reference presumably to the pines and perhaps to the occasional glimpse of a deer, but it was all at least a century too late.

The parish church of All Saints is contemporary with the railway station, both pieces of architecture possessing some merit without being very much out of the ordinary. The latter is not actually in Crowborough at all but a good mile and a half down the hill towards Rotherfield at Jarvis Brook. Traditionally this was the home of gypsies, of whom a good many remain, living in permanent houses on a council estate erected at the time of the Second World War. "They're the ones who make the money today" I was told, not with any particular note of regret, by a resident on the hill who also commented, when I referred to the factory estate about to be built beside the railway, "that's the only place they'd allow it".

The population of Crowborough grew steadily, reaching 4,000 in the mid-1950s. Then came the property boom. As a result land was often more valuable than the buildings upon it, especially if they were draughty rambling Victorian or Edwardian mansions standing in extensive grounds. Estates of two, three or four bedroomed semi-detached houses sprang up in their places, save for the few that became nursing homes—Conan Doyle's house, for example, became the Horder Centre for Arthritics—and now Crowborough, whilst barely increasing in area, has quadrupled in population. One more large estate housing some 4,000 people has been approved and if the present shortage of funds proves temporary, the town will then reach its planned ceiling of 20,000.

The Ashdown Forest, into which Crowborough has encroached, is the largest remnant of the great forest which once totally filled the Weald and extended 120 miles from Kent through Sussex into Hampshire. The motorist on the A22 London to Eastbourne road can have no doubt he has left Surrey and the furthest reaches of suburbia once he is past Forest Row, for he finds himself driving through the heart of the forest, the branches of the trees on either side reaching over to form a tunnel through which he ascends for two miles to the summit at Wych Cross. From there the road continues along on the same level but is still encompassed about with trees for another mile and a half until it comes out to an area of gorse and bushes, beyond which extend glorious views across the forest to Kent, St Leonards Forest west of the Brighton Road, and the blue-grey ridge of the South Downs.

One of my earliest and most vivid memories of the Ashdown Forest is of driving through it in a downpour. We had been to visit an old friend of my father, they had served together in Palestine in the First World War. He was a gardener in a big house near Maresfield and bore the singularly appropriate name of Herb Ashdown. The car was a 1932 Lanchester Ten with a fabric roof, and so heavily did the rain beat down through the trees that it found its way through the seams in the roof and I had to cover my head with my mackintosh.

We drove all over Sussex in that old Lanchester. My father bought it for practically nothing from a dealer whose premises were a couple of front gardens on Brixton Hill. It needed a fair amount of attention, but my father, who had trained as a mechanic working on Daimlers immediately before the First World War, and in the 1920s and '30s had worked as a chauffeur at a number of big houses in Sussex and elsewhere, had more than three years to get it roadworthy; petrol for private motoring being unobtainable during the war. Our first long trip was, inevitably, to Brighton. Later we had a weekend when we slept in the car on Winchelsea Beach and got stuck behind a convoy of army lorries heading out of Rye across the Marshes into Kent. We went to Newhaven, which my mother thought was a miserable place because there was no proper beach and it looked very rundown after the war, but my father and I liked it because of the rickety bridge and the ships. The following summer we spent a week in a chalet at Pagham and thus within a couple of years our old Lanchester opened up Sussex to me.

The first recorded appearance of the name Ashdown is in 1371, when it was granted to John of Gaunt as part of the properties of the Duchy of Lancaster, at which time it also acquired the title Lancaster Great Park. It is, however, very much older than this. There is a Bronze Age tumulus at Gills Lap east of Wych Cross, and an Iron Age camp at West Hoathly; and Alfred fought and defeated the Danes somewhere in the forest—Dane Hill is a village three miles south of Wych Cross. The Roman road from London to Lewes entered the forest at Hartfield, ran approximately parallel to the modern B2026 through Fairwarp, and continued on west of Maresfield and Uckfield.

In John of Gaunt's time Ashdown Forest covered some 14,000 acres and it was during this period that it was enclosed. Pedestrians were allowed through gaps, known as hatches—hence Coleman's Hatch and Church Hatch (Forest Row was once Walhill Hatch)—but barriers prevented the deer which John of Gaunt hunted from escaping. There were many who objected to the fencing off of the forest and to this day there are disputes about ownership and rights. There was a good deal of farmland within the enclosure, much of which survived in the hands of smallholders until it was sold for building plots fifty to

The A22 in the Ashdown Forest

The Ashdown Forest

50

sixty years ago at the time Crowborough was expanding; although there was also some development along the northern fringes and beside the A22. John of Gaunt's deer, or rather their descendants, are still to be found in the forest, although the only time I have seen one near the A22 was at night, dead. It must have been startled and had leapt out in front of a car and been killed; the driver must have had a terrible fright. There are signs outside Forest Row and south of Nutley warning motorists to keep a look-out for these creatures, but there is precious little one can do when a deer suddenly appears out of the black night into the headlights.

Down the hill from Wych Cross is a Scout camp situated on 100 acres of land given by Alfred R. Wagg of East Grinstead in 1928, his original intention being that city boys should be given a taste of country life. When it opened in 1930, a hundred and fifty sons of working men from east and south London were the first occupants. It was about this time (in July 1929 to be precise) that a tremendous pageant took place in Ashdown Forest, devised by Lord Edward Gleichen, who lived nearby, and held in Kidbrooke Park on the edge of the forest.

It told in nine episodes its history from the Ancient Britons down to the present time and must have been a remarkable occasion—there are people living in and around the forest who still speak of it—bringing together a wealth of talent. Victoria Sackville-West wrote the pro-logue, which was spoken by 'the Spirit of Anderida', a role which was to have been played by Sybil Thorndike until she fell ill. Amongst the audience were Rudyard Kipling and the present Queen Mother, then Duchess of York. The Southern Railway issued special cheap day-tickets to Forest Row at half the normal fare and a great many took advantage of the offer. The final episode is described in *The Enchanted Places*, the autobiography of the principal player, Christopher Milne. He was nine years old at the time, the only son of A. A. Milne, and as Christopher Robin was probably the best known child of his age. His part in the pageant entailed walking down through the trees into the central arena carrying the toys which his father's books had made famous; Pooh, Piglet, Eeyore, Tigger, Kanga and the rest.

'The Enchanted Places' were the northern edges of the forest, for in 1925 the Milne family had moved to Cotchford Farm, half a mile south of Hartfield, and in the next few years they were immortalized both in Milne's writings and in the drawings of E. H. Shepherd. Many of them are easily identifiable; easiest of all, perhaps, the clump of pine trees known in reality as Gills Leap, and in the books as 'Galleons Lap', which is situated at the summit of the slope up from Hartfield a little to the west of the B2026.

I have talked to people who knew the Milnes, including the present occupants of Mitchell's garage, where they now renovate old military vehicles—an extension, perhaps, of Mr Mitchell's work on Christopher Milne's pistol—and whilst the family certainly did not go out of their way to court popularity there was a constant stream of visitors. Milne wrote only four books for children, the last of which, *The House at Pooh Corner*, was published in 1928, and he valued his plays and books for adults much more highly although they were vastly less successful. Mrs Milne lived on at Hartfield after her husband's death; one of her neighbours and friends of later years was Lady Lutyens, the architect's wife. Since her death the house has changed hands several times. One of the owners was Brian Jones of 'The Rolling Stones', and it was in a pool in the garden that he died.

Another writer who lived at Hartfield for many years was Ivan Margary, the acknowledged authority on the Roman occupation of southern England. His book *Roman Roads in the Weald* produced much new evidence on the subject. Just north of Hartfield, at Holtye, Margary excavated a section of the London to Lewes road and in 1939 made it over to the Sussex Archaeological Society. A fenced-off section has been left exposed and it is possible to see the grooves worn by cart-wheels in the paving stone 1700 years ago.

One of the attractions of Britain for the Romans was iron, and one of the centres of the iron industry was the Ashdown Forest. The seemingly unlimited supply of wood encouraged its promotion for a thousand years and more, but in time, as the expanse of open gorse and scrub grew and the trees continued to be felled, the industry faltered and was finally brought to an end in the eighteenth century. Relics are few and hard to find, but they do exist, and one summer afternoon I set out to find the site of an ironworks beneath Crowborough Beacon. I had with me the standard work on the subject, Straker's *Wealden Iron*, and thus knew that a mill, also now abandoned, had been subsequently built on the site, but even so my search was hardly straightforward. Striking out southwards from the Crowborough to Withyham road I had first to choose from a number of diverging paths. Picking the most likely-looking I followed it through the bracken for over a mile, into a wood, climbed a gate, continued beside a stream which proved to be a false trail, and finally turned eastward beside another much narrower stream. To keep beside it I had to abandon the well-used track and edge along an overgrown path, through high nettles and briars. But the effort was rewarded by a sudden break in the dense mass of branches and foliage, revealing a clearing and an amount of tumble-down masonry and brickwork. Through it ran the stream and in the stream were small pieces of iron.

It would be tempting to claim that this iron was from the old works but of course it could hardly have been so. The timber-mill had quite obliterated any such possibility, but it is less fanciful to suppose that the extensive brick-work lying in ruins about the clearing might have incorporated material from the forge. What was certainly true of that Sussex wood, silent on that warm July afternoon, was that men had dug iron from beneath it and had cast it into cannon and shot for the ships of Elizabeth I's navy. Eventually the forge had ceased production and the ironworks had moved on elsewhere. I was now looking at all that remained of the timber-mill which had succeeded it, yet in essence the scene in the clearing amongst the oak and the ash trees, with the undergrowth encroaching upon the tumbled brick and the rusty iron in the stream, was no different from the one which would have confronted me 300 years before had I come upon it in the dying days of the ironworks.

For centuries iron dominated the economy of Sussex and the products of the ironworks went to the four corners of the earth. There is evidence that it existed more than 2,000 years ago, and Julius Caesar commented upon it when he landed in Britain. The Romans were the first to exploit the iron in a systematic way, setting up furnaces in the south-east of the county. Most were within fairly easy access of the port of Anderida (Pevensey). The ore was found in the clay of the Weald at a depth not greater than twenty feet and dug out from open pits, whilst the timber of the Wealden forests provided the fuel with which to smelt the ore. The combination of the rich seams of iron ore and what must in Roman times have appeared to be an inexhaustible quantity of timber provided the perfect conditions in which the industry could flourish.

The most famous product of the Sussex ironmakers was their cannon. The earliest were highly unreliable contrivances made out of leather and bound around with iron hoops. They were no doubt a fiercesome sight; the flash of flame, the great belch of smoke and the roar of the explosion as the powder was ignited must have convinced the knights on their horses that the forces of hell had been let loose upon them. But as the smoke died away those who stood their ground were as likely as not to discover that more damage had been done to the owners of the gun than to themselves. It was a frequent occurrence for the cannon to burst asunder when the powder was lit, slaughtering and maiming those operating it.

In 1543 the forge at Buxted cast the first cannon made entirely from one piece of iron, and warfare was revolutionized. The side which possessed the superiority in cannon was almost certain to carry the day. Although one-piece cannon were soon in production in Europe, such was the continuing demand from abroad for Sussex ordinance that the Government took fright and restricted exports, not wishing to find British armies at the receiving end of British-made cannon.

Through the iron industry Sussex maintained its tradition as a seafaring county. The Cinque Ports may have been in decline by the time of the Armada and able to provide only two ships for the British fleet which opposed it, but by way of compensation it was Sussex cannon which did much of the damage to the Spaniards. In the sixteenth and seventeenth centuries the county had a virtual monopoly in supplying cannon for the Royal Navy, a monopoly which lasted until 1760 when the contract passed to Scotland.

The defeat of the Armada brought about the end of the boom years for the ironmakers. At its height it is reckoned that around 7,000 men, probably rather more than one in ten of the male working population, were engaged in producing Sussex iron. An order went out from the Government to cease casting guns and in the relatively peaceful years which followed little such work came the way of the Sussex forges. Iron had many other uses and the manufacture of tools, needles, arrowheads, tombstones, forebacks and much else continued; but the great days were over. By the early eighteenth century hardly twenty furnaces and forges remained in operation, and the very last working forge, at Ashburnham near Battle, shut down in 1828, having operated but fitfully in its last years.

Imported iron has continued to be worked in Sussex, both on a small scale in village and farm smithies, and in large foundries. The best known of the latter is the Sussex Engineering Company of Lewes, which was founded in 1835 as the Phoenix Ironworks. When the firm celebrated its centenary the great-grandson of the founder, John Every, was at its head. It donated a number of iron seats for the use of the public in Lewes, and displayed some of its world-famous products in a museum on the premises. The new bridge across the Ouse passes close by the foundry and is named the Phoenix Causeway.

On a small scale, shepherds' crooks are still made in Sussex. The oldest ones, some made from melted-down cannon, are collectors' pieces, as no doubt modern ones (notably those produced at Pyecombe) will one day become.

It might reasonably be thought that an industry which had lasted for 2,000 years and which disappeared within the last 200 would have left behind substantial remains, but it is probably true to say that there are more Roman structures still standing in Sussex than there are those associated with the iron industry. The walls of Pevensey and Chichester were built on a massive scale and still served a purpose long after their creators had gone; a furnace for extracting iron was, on the other hand, a roughly made affair, easily demolished, and even the forges where the iron was shaped and manufactured were in many cases no larger than a village blacksmith's shop. When the ironmaking ceased they had one last function to perform for the community, that of providing bricks for other buildings.

East Grinstead, north of the Ashdown Forest, and in the

East Grinstead from the south, with St Swithin's prominent

heart of what was once iron country, is administratively in West Sussex, although I can never get used to this for it seems to belong so much to the east. It is within three miles of the Kent border, stands astride the most easterly of the main roads, the A22, which link London, Surrey and the coast, and overlooks the source of that symbol of Kent, the Medway. The Medway actually flows for some twelve miles through Sussex and the last 2½ of these, in the vicinity of Groombridge, forms the border between Sussex and Kent. The precise location of its source is disputed, some claiming it to be at a pond at Turner's Hill, others a mile or so to the north in a thickly wooded area close beside the abandoned East Grinstead to Three Bridges railway line known as Butcher's Wood. That the origin of so celebrated a river is obscure is not as surprising as it might initially seem, for many streams rise hereabouts, and indeed Robert H. Goodsall in his *The Medway and its Tributaries* recounts a meeting with a local inhabitant who assured him that what the Ordnance Survey claimed was the source of the Medway was actually that of the Ouse.

The Medway forms a valley between the ridge on which East Grinstead stands and the Ashdown Forest, and one sometimes has the feeling that Sussex does not really begin until one is across the river, and that East Grinstead is a frontier post in no-man's-land holding back fierce hordes of suburbanites flourishing rolled umbrellas and wheeled shopping-baskets, rampant after their triumphs over Oxted and Lingfield. This is reinforced by the London Country buses which reach East Grinstead and Forest Row from Croydon, and the commuter-line from Victoria which terminates in the town. At one time East Grinstead Station was an impressive affair on two levels, with lines radiating to Three Bridges, Haywards Heath, Lewes, Eridge, Tunbridge Wells and London. Now only the London line remains and the old Victorian station was bought by an American and replaced by a cleaner if less extensive modern one a few years back. The handsome brick viaduct at the south-western end remains, although the tracks it carries across the valley serve only as sidings; one day steam trains may rumble across it again for the Bluebell Railway has plans to relay the track northwards from Horsted Keynes and for this reason has bought the site of the intermediate station at West Hoathly.

During the Second World War a train approaching East Grinstead was attacked by a German aircraft, and the town suffered a good deal from enemy action, the worst incident being in 1943 when a cinema, along with shops and houses, was bombed. In all, 108 people died. There is a memorial to them in the parish church, together with another commemorating three others killed by a flying bomb a year later. East Grinstead's best known contribution to the war effort is the Royal Victoria Hospital where aircrew and others who had suffered burns were cared for. The war memorial chapel in the parish church dates from 1920; later the names of the Second World War victims were added, along with the ensign of the Royal Canadian Air Force, "presented in gratitude" in 1945.

Although the town has a long history—the "Hundred of Grenestede" is mentioned in the *Domesday Book*—and is known to have been a borough since at least 1235, the parish church is less than 200 years old. Tradition has it that the first building on the site was a wooden one, erected to give shelter to the body of Edward the Confessor on its way to Westminster Abbey in 1066. In time, a more substantial one took its place and was rebuilt at various times, but in 1785 it was almost totally destroyed when the tower collapsed, causing the walls of the nave to come down too. Known for a long time as St Swithun's (after a ninth-century Bishop of Winchester), although dedicated to St Edmund, the church stands on the highest point in the town at the southern end. The 100 foot-high tower is a notable landmark and can be seen for many miles around, across the Kent and Surrey borders.

There are a number of handsome buildings lining the south end of the High Street in the vicinity of St Swithun's, and some alms-houses to the east, beyond the church, which date from 1616 and are known as Sackville College, after the family which had owned the living since 1554. The High Street, which is the A22, makes an almost ninety-degree turn and becomes narrower and busier and loses most of its character, the buildings from here onwards being nondescript examples of nineteenth- and twentieth-century architecture. Whilst the traffic through East Grinstead seldom gets itself into quite such a tangle as it does in Uckfield, it can be pretty bad, and the relief road now under construction along the old railway line is much needed, unlike the vast office blocks standing beside it, empty ever since they were built four years ago.

East Grinstead still has a cinema, sufficiently profitable to have been turned into three smaller ones; and there is also a theatre, the Adelene Genee, which is actually a few hundred yards inside the Surrey border, over which the northern suburbs of East Grinstead now spill. The cattle-market has gone, but there is still a market for farm produce and agricultural implements as well as general merchandise. A relic of former days is a notice informing the public that no one may remove a pig without a licence; a remote possibility unless one counts pork sausages and bacon sandwiches.

Crawley emerged from the obscurity of a Wealden iron-producing settlement into a place of some importance in the latter part of the eighteenth century. Situated roughly half-way between London and Brighton, it was a convenient spot to change horses. The most famous of the coaching inns, The George, featured in a Rowlandson print and is still standing, albeit altered a good deal; the

The Boulevard, Crawley

58

London end of the road having most of its original buildings.

The railway by-passed Crawley, the road which had once been so busy became no more than a muddy track, and the town went into a fifty-year-long decline. The motor car reversed this and Crawley's fortunes revived, which was something of a mixed blessing, for by the 1930s the High Street became almost impassable on summer weekends and the hospital had to be enlarged to cope with the number of casualties from motoring accidents.

Yet even in the years just after the Second World War, an outing to the seaside by car was still considered sufficiently novel and adventurous for Crawley shopkeepers to benefit from the numbers who felt it necessary to break their journey half-way, and many will remember the café where Southdown coaches stopped to refresh their passengers at the mid-way point of their journey to the sea. Now of course not only is there a by-pass but a motorway and through traffic has long since avoided the town centre.

The congestion has not been greatly eased, however, for the year after the Second World War ended, the Attlee government passed a Bill which has transformed Crawley to a greater extent than any of the previous turnabouts in its fortunes. This was the New Town Act, which extended the idea of the garden city and created eight new towns in a ring twenty to thirty miles from London. Only one was south of the river; Crawley. Designed principally to house Londoners made homeless during the bombing or displaced by slum clearance, from the outset it was intended that there would be sufficient jobs within the New Town for all its inhabitants. At the same time its proximity to the A23 and the main line at Three Bridges ensured that they would have no trouble maintaining their links with their old homes.

For all that, the upheaval for those who had lived all their lives in a close-knit community in the East End was considerable. Some had never before travelled as great a distance as the thirty-one miles from Victoria to Crawley, and there were children who looked out of the carriage windows at the fields and asked which were the sheep and which were the cows. Their old homes may have been bad and lacking in many of what would now be considered the essential amenities, yet some of Crawley New Town's first inhabitants would have much preferred to have stayed where they were. Those responsible for its creation and administration knew this and did their best to make the transition as painless as possible; and of course there were many who right from the start welcomed the chance of a new beginning.

By early 1950 the first thirty-two houses and flats were ready. One hundred and five more homes were to be built initially on a ten-acre site; the homes being of eighteen different types with from one to five bedrooms. The Crawley Development Corporation was responsible for the over-all design, but individual variations were allowed and it was hoped that the tenants would express opinions about their homes so that improvements could be incorporated. Whilst this was going on work started on the industrial estate alongside the A23.

To the north of Crawley, just across the Surrey border, was Gatwick Aerodrome. It was small and used only by a handful of private flyers. Immediately after the war there had been plans for absorbing the adjoining racecourse and turning it into something very much larger, but about the time Crawley New Town was set up it was announced that such an airport would have been "quite incompatible with the proper development of the new town".

Almost all the early homes in Crawley were owned by the council, rents ranging from 15s. to 30s. 9d. per week. Half the new tenants had never rented a complete house or flat before, and practically all of them came from London, in equal numbers from the L.C.C. and the outer suburban areas. As initially designed, Crawley was to have no flats of more than three storeys, no part of the town would be more than one mile from open country, but at the same time everyone would live near enough to his work to be able to come home at lunchtime if he wished. In these and other ways the care that had gone into the design of the New Town was obvious. It was developed out of three communities already in existence: Crawley, and the villages of Ifield and Three Bridges. In 1946 the combined population of the three was a little under 10,000. It was planned that it should increase fourfold.

Gradually Crawley developed. The acres of muddy building-sites became rows of neat houses; by 1951 seven factories, all formerly based in London, were in production; in 1952 the first prefabricated school was opened; and the town centre sported the "attractive and unusual feature" of a pedestrian thoroughfare. By 1956, the number of rented homes which were occupied was 6,200 328 had been sold privately; 76 factories were in business, there were 5 churches or church halls, 6 community buildings, 2 pubs, a crematorium, 1 almost completed fire station, 26 town centre shops, 73 neighbourhood ones, 6 neighbourhood centres, 3,840 primary school places, 750 secondary modern ones, and 540 in the new grammar school. Ninety per cent of its new population was under 45 years of age, there was a long waiting list of grandparents who wished to retire to Crawley from London, and already with its total population up to 30,000, Crawley was the largest inland town in Sussex.

Today this figure is 70,000; and Crawley not only outstrips anywhere else in inland Sussex but also all the seaside towns, with the exceptions of Eastbourne and Hastings (it is on a par with the latter), Worthing and Brighton. The raw newness of the early 1950s has worn off and its shopping centre, with a much extended pedestrian precinct, attracts people from far beyond the town's boundaries.

The greatest change in emphasis since the early days has been the move away from rented accommodation; by the end of 1974 almost half the houses were owner-occupied. Parking is a considerable problem, for there was originally little accommodation for cars and the present high land values do not encourage the building of garages which can be rented at a rate people can afford.

Whilst there is no outstanding architecture in Crawley—a lost opportunity of considerable proportions—Queen's Square in the heart of the town serves its purpose very well. The absence of vehicles, the abundance of mature trees, the bandstand (rescued from the old Gatwick racecourse) and the fountains, make it a centre which really works. Housewives meet and talk whilst out shopping, children play safely and old people sit and watch.

Recreational facilities are provided in Crawley on a more lavish scale than in many older towns, there being 690 acres of parks and open spaces, a cinema (a relic of the pre-New Town Crawley) with an entertainment centre next door, a sports centre, a swimming pool where international matches are staged, and many youth clubs, play groups, etc.

Gatwick Airport, which the old Development Corporation was assured would never be built, is now the second busiest in the country and provides work for many people in Crawley.

The town is still growing. The Strategic Plan for the South East envisages an enormous complex of new towns, enlarged old ones, villages and intervening countryside, with a total population of a quarter-million, of which Crawley would form the northern section. Sussex cannot stagnate, and a home within it remains the laudable desire of a good many people at present living elsewhere. But if much more of the countryside disappears, with it goes much of the county's attraction, and one may hope that any further expansion of Crawley is kept to a minimum and carried out with the greatest care.

62   *The Carfax, Horsham*

CHAPTER FOUR

Horsham to Midhurst

Horsham is a town which in recent years has undergone a greater transformation than any in Sussex, other than Crawley. It has been a place of importance for a thousand years, it was mentioned in a Saxon land charter in 947 and referred to as a borough in 1235. It sent its first member to Parliament in 1295. The arrival of the railway in 1848 put it within easy reach of London and it is now connected to the capital by two routes, each served by a frequent service of fast trains. A great many people live in Horsham and work in London and a great many more drive through the town each day in their cars. The ancient centre is the Carfax, a more or less circular area, with a group of buildings in a smaller circle in the bottom south-west corner, a nice Victorian bandstand, and what used to be a severe traffic problem. The continuing growth of the town, both in its own right and as an overspill of Crawley, throughout the 1950s and '60s eventually provoked a drastic redevelopment of the entire area immediately north of the Carfax. This was largely Victorian and it was swept away to be replaced by a road system which has certainly justified its existence by taking away all but local traffic from the Carfax. There is a multi-storey car park, new office blocks and, best of all, a shopping centre built to a human scale and making considerable use of local brick and matching wood. Dominating Swan Square, at the heart of the precinct (the foundation stone of which was laid by the Duke of Norfolk in December 1973) and just visible from the Carfax, is an enormous gold clock-face.

Very different in style but universally admired is the Causeway, which extends from behind the south side of the Carfax to the parish church of St Mary. The first house on the left, built in the early 1600s, is the home of the Horsham Museum Society and is notable for its reconstructions of a nineteenth-century forge, a tannery, a creamery, and an eighteenth-century kitchen. There is also a collection of other relics: old bicycles, a model of a windmill, stuffed animals and an entertainingly eccentric jumble typical of a country town museum. A number of the buildings in the Causeway sport neat labels bearing brief details of their histories, put up by the Horsham Festival Committee in 1975.

The parish church of St Mary the Virgin once belonged to the nuns of Rusper, a village north of Horsham on the Surrey border, and was largely rebuilt by them in the reign of King John. The nunnery was dissolved by Henry

The brickworks at Southwater, one of the homes of Horsham bricks

VIII, by which time all but some fragments of the original church had been replaced in the thirteenth century with some fourteenth- and fifteenth-century additions; inevitably it was restored by enthusiastic but heavy-handed Victorians. The tower contains most of the remaining work of the twelfth and thirteenth centuries, surmounted by the $156\frac{1}{2}$-foot-high spire covered in 50,000 wooden shingles.

Particularly pleasant is the view down the Causeway, past the old houses and the handsome church, to the churchyard, the Garden of Remembrance, the Arun, and the open country beyond. It always comes as something of a surprise to rediscover in what is now a large and still-growing town that the country extends to within a few hundred yards of its centre.

The main shopping street, West Street, extending from the Carfax, has become a pedestrian precinct, and is a continuation of the narrow Middle Street, which has been pedestrianized for rather longer, and the equally miniature Market Square which contains the Duke of Norfolk's Town Hall. The heart of Horsham has not greatly changed in the thirty odd years I have known it, but beyond the Carfax it is very different. The Capitol Theatre is now engulfed by the new car parks, roads and shopping centre, its mock-Grecian façade looking very out of place although internally it is unaffected and remains neat and cosy. Northwards past the rather splen-

did St Mark's of 1870 are the council offices and the railway station with its functional and now dated rebuilt front of 1938. The narrow and heavily used bridge leads past the sidings and a timber yard and into an extensive development of houses. Another new road cuts through these which stretch away, row after row on either side, for the best part of two miles as far as Roffey, a Victorian suburb with a very suburban-looking parish church, All Saints, designed by Blomfield a 100 years ago. Once past Roffey is the country with wooded slopes leading up to the Surrey border to the north, Tilgate Forest to the south, and Crawley to the east.

West of Horsham is Christ's Hospital, another late Victorian development, albeit a very different one from the terraces of Roffey. Money must have been virtually unlimited when the move was being planned from the City of London in the 1890s, for the elaborate buildings cover a considerable area and are set in very spacious grounds. The school took nine years to complete and there have been a number of additions over the years. The traditional uniform worn by the boys—black cassock and breeches and yellow stockings—is a familiar sight in and around Horsham. As with all boarding-schools, the visitor to Christ's Hospital cannot but be aware of the air of claustrophobia, which is inevitable where a large number of people work, eat, sleep and find their entertainment in close proximity. Perhaps it is the masters and their families

Christ's Hospital

66

who are most in danger of losing their identities, for many of the teachers devote most of their time and sometimes all of their careers to the school.

Perhaps it is with an awareness of the need to look outwards that Christ's Hospital has recently opened an arts centre, which cost £1 million, for the use of the community as much as the school. It is an enlightened move, the focal point of the complex being a 600-seat theatre, an award-winning piece of architecture which is one of the finest buildings in the county. Designed by the late Bill Howell and completed in 1974, it is in many ways a re-creation of an Elizabethan theatre. It is circular, fitted out in red-coloured wood with three galleries and a stage which can be adapted to many forms and used in a variety of guises. Entertainments and cultural events, ranging from exhibitions of paintings, prints, sculpture, etc., to performances of ballet, concerts, films and plays, are regularly put on, some specifically for children, and attracting audiences from all over the South-East.

The original Christ's Hospital buildings are a handsome mixture of Gothic and Elizabethan styles in pale red and white. They incorporate a few pieces of the earlier buildings which were brought from London, notably a section by Wren which is built into the west wall of the chapel. Inside the latter is a series of murals by Brangwyn. He may have had his limitations as a painter but Brangwyn's figures at Christ's Hospital have a vitality and humanity rarely found in an English place of worship.

The guide book describes the parish church of St Mary in Billingshurst as standing "high above the village", but Billingshurst has always seemed to me to be a town, a small but important place mid-way between Horsham and Pulborough where the main road to Bognor crosses the ancient route from Winchester to Canterbury, now the A272. Although Billingshurst is not mentioned in the *Domesday Book* its site was known to the Romans, for it lies on Stane Street on the long section which is still in use as the A29 London to Bognor road. The earliest mention of it is in a charter of 1293 where the name "Richard atte Stanstrete of Slinfold and Billingshurst" occurs. The first church at Billingshurst was probably built about 100 years before this, the oldest pieces remaining being a doorway and lancet windows in the south wall, and parts of the tower, all of which date to around 1220. St Mary's stands at the south end of the town at the bottom of the gently sloping main street and overlooking its junction with the A272.

For the rest of this chapter we will follow the A272 which will take us through some of the best scenery that Sussex has to offer, into two historic towns, and gradually closer to the South Downs until we are within a couple of miles of them at the Hampshire border.

Two miles west of Billingshurst is the appropriately named Wisborough Green, the village green being one of

West Chiltington, near Billingshurst

the largest in Sussex. The road curves around the bank upon which the handsome church stands, crosses one side of the green, passes the minute Zoar Chapel of 1753, and winds through wooded country until, within sight of Petworth, it straightens, dips and finally ascends into the town which stands against the sky in a bold, almost forbidding manner.

Up to a point Petworth is to West Sussex what Rye is to East Sussex, being set on a hill and full of handsome old buildings. Beyond this the parallel ends, for Petworth is very much an inland town, not all the buildings are as perfectly preserved as in Rye—there are less visitors—and despite its elevated setting it does not stand alone but is dominated by a great house and its grounds.

Bedevilling Petworth for some years now has been its traffic problem. Its narrow streets are incapable of handling the traffic; five through routes from Midhurst, Guildford, Billingshurst, Pulborough and Chichester disgorge into them and neither of the two proposed solutions please everyone. One would involve demolishing a number of buildings of note at the southern end of the town; the other would drive a by-pass through the grounds of Petworth House. Such is the historic importance of the town, the house and its park that discussion and lobbying for and against the alternatives has spread far beyond Sussex. The cut-back in public spending has held up work for the present, although the most likely solution and the most

humane—in that it would not cause the eviction of anyone from his home—is the park one, possibly by way of a tunnel. It would certainly be a great shame if the superb view across the park from the house to the Downs, planned by Capability Brown and painted by Turner and Constable, should be disfigured.

Petworth House is one of the grandest in the county, being chiefly the creation of the sixth Duke of Somerset, who extensively rebuilt and added to it towards the end of the seventeenth century. The Duke thought so highly of himself that he took great offence at any who failed to share his enthusiasm and deprived one of his unfortunate daughters of her inheritance when he fell asleep and awoke to find her sitting down instead of standing as a mark of respect. Greater men have lesser monuments, and the sixth Duke is fortunate that he is remembered chiefly for creating Petworth, doubly so as the architect is unknown. His son was the last Duke of Somerset, the ownership of Petworth passing on his death to a nephew, Charles Wyndham, second Earl of Egremont. The third Earl succeeded to the title and the house at the age of twelve in 1763. It is fitting that he should be the best remembered of Petworth's owners for by all accounts he was an unusually kind and cultured man. He held the title for sixty-five years, dying in the year of Queen Victoria's accession. In his own way his relationship with his family was as eccentric as that of his ancestor, for although there seems to have

A view of Petworth from the A272 from the east

been no reason why they should not have married he and a Miss Iliffe preferred to produce six illegitimate children before they finally took the plunge and made their union legal. The resultant shock was apparently so great that they parted two years later after a seventh, legitimate child had been born.

Lord Egremont was the friend of some of the most famous politicians of his time, although his greatest enthusiasm was for the arts. Many painters stayed in his house and on the cover of the guidebook to Petworth is a picture by one of them—William Frederick Witherington—of a fête in the grounds. On such occasions as many as 10,000 people, most of them local farmers and farm workers, would attend, and the kitchens would be called upon to roast more than 1,000 stones of meat and boil 1,000 plum puddings. Turner and Constable both attended these festivities and it is recorded that Constable was much taken with the spectacular effects a fireworks display created in the night sky at the culmination of one particular jamboree.

Constable is always associated with East Anglia and it is certainly that part of the world for which he had the greatest affection. But he spent little time there in his later years, living in London and frequently visiting Petworth and elsewhere in Sussex. Of the South Downs and the Weald he was driven to exclaim "I have never seen such scenery as your country affords; I prefer it to anything for my pictures." His very last painting was *Arundel Mill and Castle*. He was working on it the day he died and it was left unfinished. Earlier, in 1824, whilst living with his family at Brighton, Constable wrote less favourably of the county, "In short there is nothing here for a painter but the breakers . . . and sky . . . which have been lovely indeed and always varying. The fishing-boats are picturesque but not so much as the Hastings boats, which are luggers . . . But these subjects are so hackneyed . . ." Perhaps they were, but Constable transformed them, and with a deceptive facility captured the effect of the wind upon the waves and the clouds in so perfect a manner that each time one looks at a picture such as *Brighton Beach*, in the Victoria and Albert Museum, one is almost surprised to find there is no spray upon one's face and one waits, half-expecting to see the sun break through a patch of blue in the sky.

Turner's associations with Petworth and Sussex are even stronger. He had his own studio in Petworth House and spent some of the happiest days of his not-always-happy life in the company of Lord Egremont and the many children who inhabited or visited Petworth. By the 1830s Turner was producing paintings which were truly revolutionary; many of his contemporaries thought them the works of a once-great artist's declining years, and not even the French Impressionists fifty years later took the study of the effects of light further than he. More widely travelled than Constable, Turner needed the fierce sun of

Lodsworth, a village close to the A272 between Petworth and Midhurst

71

Italy and the Mediterranean to reveal to him what shimmering, magical effects of sky and sea he could create, but in his studio at Petworth he carried this revelation into all his pictures. One of his most famous is the *Interior at Petworth*, now in the Tate Gallery. So great is its concern with colour and light and so little with the mass of detail one would expect to find in a painting of a room belonging to a rich aristocrat that it is no wonder that even into the twentieth century the picture puzzled, disturbed and annoyed many critics and connoisseurs.

Lord Egremont first commissioned Turner in 1810, but the painter had been familiar with Sussex long before then. Born in London, his first recorded visit to the county of Sussex was in 1793, at the age of 18. Three years later, whilst in Brighton, he filled thirty pages of his sketchbook and then moved on to Chichester where he made further studies. From 1829 until Egremont's death in 1837, the Sussex seaside and the countryside in the vicinity of the South Downs was as great a source of inspiration to Turner as Venice had been some years earlier. He produced pictures of Rye, Winchelsea, Hastings (his *Line Fishing off Hastings* was exhibited at the Royal Academy in 1835), Arundel, Chichester and especially the grounds and vicinity of Petworth.

Thirteen Turner paintings remain at Petworth. They form a collection which any other house in the country might well envy. Gathered together in one room, they are approached along the length of the West Front through rooms full of pictures by Bosch, Van Dyck, Lely, Reynolds and other masters. These are splendid paintings, and some are all but priceless, yet one is tempted to give them less than one's full attention and hurry past, drawn towards the room at the far end of the house where the light and colour contained within Turner's thirteen masterpieces glows so brilliantly.

The south wall of the Petworth estate extends for over a mile along the A272 as far as the village of Tillington; on the opposite side of the road the Weald slopes gently away to the Downs. A handsome barn stands by itself in a field above the road to the north, beyond which is the 919-foot-high summit of Blackdown, the highest point in Sussex. Tennyson had a house near the summit; 8,000 years earlier Middle Stone Age man lived on the hill above the forest and some of the flint tools used during this period have been excavated. In Elizabethan times Blackdown was a beacon and during the seventeenth century it was a quarry, but now the 600 acres of high sandstone ridge belong to the National Trust and are a great favourite with walkers. Dark pines and heather probably account for Blackdown's name, although the soil also is very dark on the western slopes.

Midhurst, six miles west of Petworth and the most north-westerly town in Sussex, is within a couple of miles of the South Downs and not much more than twice that

72

The view south from Blackdown

Polo at Cowdray

distance from Blackdown. The main street (running north–south along the A272 and the A286 Guildford to Chichester roads) is wide, so that, unlike Petworth, there is room for the traffic to flow freely without any need for the pedestrians to feel threatened by it. At the north end is one of the most handsomely sited car parks and bus stations imaginable alongside the water meadows of the Rother (the river which separates Midhurst from the village of Easebourne) and within 100 yards of the spectacular Tudor ruins of Cowdray House.

Cowdray was begun by Owen Glendower's son in 1492, and in 1542 it passed to the second Earl of Southampton. The earl, being in Henry VIII's good books, profited from the Dissolution of the Monasteries and amongst the properties he acquired was Battle Abbey. He treated the monks with considerable discourtesy and as the last one quit the abbey he vowed its despoiler and his descendants would perish by fire and water. The curse remained in abeyance for 250 years and was then fulfilled with a vengeance. In 1793, rubbish swept up in preparation for the arrival of the young eighth earl, who was returning from Germany for his marriage, began to smoulder, the fire engine was locked away and the key could not be found, and a high wind did the rest. Eight days later the earl, who seems to have been a young man with little sense, drowned himself whilst attempting to shoot a falls on the Rhine. The culminating tragedy was the drowning of the earl's fourteen-year-old nephew and his ten-year-old brother at Bognor in 1815.

The ruins are extensive and are open to the public. One mile away is the nineteenth-century Cowdray House, owned since 1933 by the second Viscount Cowdray. A feature of the Midhurst district is the yellow ochre paint applied to the many farmhouses, cottages and other buildings which belong to the estate. It is a pleasant enough colour but its widespread application might be thought an over-strident echo of more feudal times. The superbly landscaped Cowdray Park through, which the A272 approaches Midhurst, is famous as the home of polo where the Duke of Edinburgh and Prince Charles often play.

Although there are a number of handsome buildings in the main street (North Street) of Midhurst, the finest group is to be found to the south-east up Knock Hundred Row, in Church Hill and Red Lion Street. Here the collection of mainly sixteenth-, seventeenth- and eighteenth-century buildings forms the heart of the old town. Amongst them is the library, on the corner, housed in a group of seventeenth-century timbered and tile-hung cottages; the sixteenth-century Old Market House; the Spread Eagle coaching inn, going back to 1430 and said—inevitably—to have been slept in by Elizabeth I; the half-timbered Elizabeth House; and much else of note in brick and half-timbering. The parish church of St Mary Magdalene and St Denys, restored in the nineteenth century,

75

North Street, Midhurst

76

The Market Square, Midhurst

77

stands on the east side of Market Square. A curfew bell rings at eight o'clock every evening; a tradition kept up, so it is said, to commemorate a commercial traveller who was once lost on heathland to the north of the town and was guided back by the bell. In gratitude he gave a piece of land, known as Curfew Garden and situated opposite what is now the Youth Centre, as an endowment to ensure the perpetual ringing of the bell.

South Pond, down the hill from the Market Square, was given to the townspeople by the present Lord Cowdray; he also presented St Ann's Hill, between the Market Square and the Rother and site of a castle abandoned when Cowdray House was built. Midhurst is proud of its grammar school (which is actually comprehensive), founded in 1672 in the Market Square and now situated at the north end of the town. Amongst its former pupils are Richard Cobden and H. G. Wells. The latter worked for a time in a chemist's shop in the town, putting his experiences to good use in some of his novels, notably *Tono Bungay*. Two final buildings worth noting: in North Street the Angel Hotel, which was so named by the Pilgrim Fathers who stayed there on their way to Southampton in 1620; and the new Roman Catholic Church of Holy Mary at the south end of Midhurst which although very different to anything else in the town, is perhaps not quite different enough.

The A272 leaves the A286 at the bottom of Rumbolds Hill, the continuation of North Street, and above the site of the old railway station—Midhurst was once served by three branch lines, all now vanished—and continues westwards, parallel to the Rother. Two villages, Trotton and Rogate, both worth visiting, lie on its route before the Hampshire border is reached within sight of Petersfield. The latter town, although much larger than Midhurst and, with its mainline station, a centre for the surrounding district, including a good part of West Sussex, is not as attractive as its Sussex neighbour, but it is worth following the A272 to its natural end at Winchester—although it actually continues another nine miles to the A30 at Stockbridge—if only to experience the spectacular 600-foot-summit up on the Downs above Winchester. It climbs steadily until it reaches a bare, uninhabited landscape of such wild grandeur, particularly when the wind howls across it on a grey winter day, that one might be a continent away from the lush gentle Sussex Weald half a dozen miles distant.

CHAPTER FIVE

Arundel and the Downs

There can be few areas in all of England with more to offer the historian, or indeed anyone the least interested in how we got to be the sort of people we are, than that immediately north of Chichester. On the whole it is not the more bloodthirsty sort of history but is none the less fascinating for that and extends from the beginnings of man down to the day before yesterday. Chichester itself is the longest continuously lived-in settlement in the county, and if we included it in this chapter we could easily fill half the book, so we will restrict ourselves to the downlands between the Hampshire border and the River Arun.

As far as is known the first *homo sapiens* crossed into Britain from Europe before the two were separated by the sea at a time when the chalk downs of northern France and south-eastern England were one. For a time it was thought that a skull discovered at Piltdown, near Uckfield, just before the First World War was, to quote a contemporary account, "beyond any question . . . the most ancient human remains yet found in England". A series of tests carried out in the 1950s and '60s established that the skull was a fake and the whole curious episode would seem to have been an elaborate and, for a time, highly successful hoax.

The earliest known inhabitants of Sussex were nomadic hunters of the Palaeolithic period. They had no permanent homes, grew no crops and owned no domestic animals. All they have left behind are flint tools, which they may possibly have shaped; examples have been found at Slindon, six miles north-east of Chichester.

Sometime between 6000 and 5000 B.C., when conditions in Britain were subtropical and practically no evidence of human occupation has been found in Sussex, man learnt to cultivate crops and to domesticate animals. Out of these momentous discoveries grew an ordered, cultured society of permanent settlements, of villages, of artists and craftsmen and of specialization. This civilization, centred around the eastern Mediterranean, evolved as the deserts of Mesopotamia and Egypt expanded, and it was therefore forced to move elsewhere, and around 2500 B.C. it reached Sussex. These Neolithic people lived on the Downs and from the pieces of pottery, flint implements and human and animal remains excavated from the causewayed camp at Whitehawk beside Brighton Racecourse, we know that they kept sheep, cattle, pigs and goats and almost certainly grew grain. Long barrows, or burial mounds, have been found on the Downs between Eastbourne and Brighton, and at three sites close to Chichester: Bevis's Thumb, north-west of Compton near the Hampshire border; and two at Stoughton Down to the west of the Chichester to Petersfield road.

The most perfectly preserved Neolithic remains in Sussex are the flint mines. The shafts are all filled in and can only be detected as shallow hollows, but detailed excavation at Cissbury, Church Hill, Harrow Hill and Blackpatch, all some five miles north of Worthing; and Stoke Down, Bow Hill and the Lavant Caves, north of Chichester, have shown that the shafts were up to fifty feet deep. From them, as in a coal mine, the galleries in which the actual mining was carried out opened off. Implements which have been discovered include picks made from deer antlers and shovels made from the shoulder-blades of oxen. Cecil Curwen describes the discovery of a flint mine.

> He is acutely conscious that he is the first human being to enter this underground workshop for some four thousand years . . . here and there on the walls or roof a black mark is seen. This is actually the soot from the old miners' lamps, still there and looking perfectly fresh after the lapse of 4,000 years. The great events and personages of history pass in array before our minds—William the Norman, Caesar, David, Abraham—and yet those simple soot-marks were there before them all.

The successor of Neolithic Man, Bronze Age Man, was also of Mediterranean origin but came from further west, from the Iberian Peninsula. He occupied many of the Neolithic settlements on the Downs and in these have been found the distinctive flat-bottomed pottery, or beakers, which gave rise to the 'Beaker-folk'. The Middle Bronze Age saw the introduction of cremation instead of burial, the ceremony being carried out on a barrow which consisted of a mound surrounded by a flat, circular section, this being enclosed by a ditch. Around Chichester there are three such sites; at Bow Hill, close to the flint mines; at Treyford Hill, seven miles due north of Chichester; and on Heyshott Down, five miles to the east.

The Iron Age extended into the Roman period. Again such long established settlements as Park Brow, Cissbury and Firle Beacon were used, but they were developed, and two, Cissbury and the Trundle, four miles north of Chichester, might almost be called towns. The strong iron plough enabled the heavy soils of the Weald beyond the Downs to be cultivated, and in the process large areas of trees and heathland were cleared, the first real inroads into the forests. The working of iron was perfected in Asia Minor around 1000 B.C.; it took some 900 years for the knowledge to reach Britain, the earliest evidence of mining in Sussex dating from shortly before the Roman Conquest.

The Trundle is a particularly interesting site for it was

inhabited for some 2,000 years. It was not until the 1920s, when aerial observation became possible, that the Neolithic ramparts were revealed within the Iron Age ones. Excavation of the ditches in front of the ramparts produced the remains of oxen, sheep, pigs and dogs and it is believed that by 2000 B.C. Neolithic Man was able to construct wooden towers and fortifications to augment the earthworks. Much later during the Iron Age around 400 B.C. the ramparts of the Trundle were greatly extended until the fort was some 1,500 feet across. It was abandoned during the first century B.C., although the implication in the Roman name for Chichester, *Noviomagus* (new city on the plain), is that it replaced an old one on the Downs, which could only have been the Trundle. If this is so then Chichester's origins go back to the early days of the Old Testament.

One mile north of the Trundle is the Weald and Downland Museum at Singleton, which, with a little bit of overlap, takes us on from the post-Roman era to the beginning of the present century. The Roman era itself is best left to the Chichester chapter when we can also look at Fishbourne and the roads, particularly Stane Street.

The museum was opened on a thirty-five-acre site on the edge of the Downs in 1971 and since then has gone on adding to its exhibits, providing a steadily more comprehensive picture of life in Sussex and the neighbouring counties over many centuries. The principal exhibits are buildings—houses, barns, a market hall, a smithy, a water mill and a farmhouse—all re-erected at Singleton when threatened with demolition on their original sites. They are not, however, lifeless museum pieces, but are used to illustrate the living and working conditions of the people they housed. They are designed to be seen in conjunction with the various examples of crafts and industries on display in the museum grounds. Many of these, as one might expect, are concerned with timber in one form or another.

Charcoal burning has been one of the principal industries of the Weald since earliest times. A charcoal-burner's camp has been set up by two retired burners from Horsham, Mr and Mrs Langridge. The large kiln at Singleton might take as long as three days and two nights to burn and throughout that time it would have to be watched so that the air supply was maintained and any damage made good. Because of the need for this constant attention the charcoal-burner would have his family in the camp with him. They lived in small turf huts and might stay as long as four years, eventually abandoning them; if they ever returned to the site they would build new ones. Mrs Langridge belongs to such a family and until the age of sixteen had known no other sort of home.

The charcoal industry received a boost during the Second World War when charcoal was required by gas

81

Bayleaf Farmhouse at the Open Air Museum, Singleton; threatened by a reservoir on its original site, it now stands as it was built in the sixteenth century

mask manufacturers, but although there is still a limited demand for it the traditional methods of production have largely died out. In 1939 the *Sussex County Magazine* published an account of Frank Harber who lived at Plaistow to the east of Blackdown and who was said to be the last charcoal burner in the county, although he believed there might be one other. In four days he would convert four tons of cordwood to fifteen hundredweight of charcoal. He would spend the first day setting up the kiln, the next two days burning, and the fourth day bagging the charcoal. Most of it would be sent to London grill rooms (charcoal is still produced for barbecues), the rest being used by Hatton Garden gold smelters and for blueing gun barrels. The demand was also beginning to be felt for gas mask filters but 'small' charcoal was needed for this and was produced by a less laborious process. Mr Harber had at one time produced charcoal for bootblacking and for making ink and recalled that in Tudor times at nearby Fernhurst there had been a charcoal factory which had closed down shortly after the end of Elizabeth I's continental wars, presumably with a decrease in demand for gun barrels. Until the First World War Mr Harber had lived in one of the traditional turf huts but after that time he used an old van body.

Charcoal was also used for hop-drying and in the glass industry, the latter flourishing in the Fernhurst and Plaistow districts and across the border in Surrey between the thirteenth and seventeenth centuries. The first recorded glass factory in England was at Pickhurst on the Surrey-Sussex border close to Blackdown; it is mentioned in a deed of 1226 to Laurence Vitramius of Normandy.

A third industry associated with the Fernhurst district was that of chestnut cleft fencing. Only in the South-East do chestnut trees grow in sufficient quantity for the craft to be practised. It was estimated that there were around 500 people so employed in 1939; there are a good deal less now and other types of cleft timber (that is, wood cut with an axe rather than a saw) are almost impossible to obtain. At Singleton a woodcraft area has been set up beside the charcoal burner's camp and I quote from the guide:

Cleaving still survives for certain limited purposes such as the making of chestnut palings, and the attractive post and rail fencing which is a continuing tradition in this part of the county. But the craft is dying and the museum has had considerable difficulty in finding cleft oak for the reconstruction of buildings. Cleft timber is much more durable than sawn timber since it follows the grain and minimizes the likelihood of splitting and weakness caused by cutting across the grain.

The museum has built a saw-pit, typical of the sort which existed in their hundreds until the twentieth century, although power mills had been in use in Sussex since the eighteenth century, driven first by wind or water, later by steam, and now, of course, by electricity. The master sawyer stood at the top, his assistant down in the pit, and such working conditions fully explain the reputation sawyers acquired for being hard-drinking men.

Although the Downland Museum is of recent origin, the village of Singleton is mentioned, as *Silletone*, in the *Domesday Book*. It was not, however, until the latter part of the nineteenth century that it acquired fame. In 1880 the Midhurst to Chichester branch line opened and Singleton acquired a station. A mile or south of the village is Goodwood Racecourse ('glorious Goodwood") opened on top of the Downs by the Duke of Richmond in 1802. It had long been a favourite with society and the convenience of having a station just down the hill was quickly exploited. Thus, for some forty years until the motor car put it out of business, it played host to a great number of elevated people, the most lofty of all being Edward VII and his court.

The Goodwood Estate came into the possession of the Duke of Richmond (a natural son of Charles II) in 1720 and the small brick house then existing was enlarged on several occasions, principally by James Wyatt between 1790 and 1800, although it is not generally considered one of his most successful efforts, the exterior lacking both elegance and a sense of grandeur. The grounds, on the other hand, are splendid, with fine views through the trees to Chichester and the sea. There was a motor-racing circuit here for eighteen years—the British Grand Prix was held at it—but spectator problems became so acute in the 1960s that it had to be closed to the public. It now serves as a research track. There is also an airfield, used by a club and a school of flying, within the grounds of Goodwood.

Within sight of both Chichester and Goodwood, situated between Stane Street and the A27 coast road, is Boxgrove Priory which Ian Nairn calls "the most important Early English building, after Chichester Cathedral, in Sussex". The village dates back to Saxon times; the priory to the early twelfth century when three monks from Lessay, south of Cherbourg, began the community on a site given to the Lessay Abbey by the sister of the Earl of Arundel. At the Dissolution of the Monasteries the priory was abandoned, the monks at Lessay remaining until the French Revolution. Centuries later the old links were revived when the present Vicar of Boxgrove travelled to Lessay in 1965 and addressed the congregation in the twelfth-century church there, badly damaged in 1944 but subsequently restored. Most of the domestic buildings at Boxgrove are gone or are overgrown, story-book romantic-looking ruins, but the church, although not much more than half its original size, is now beautifully cared for. The twelfth-century nave is a ruin, but the present nave, built around 1220 as the choir, is a splendid replacement featuring Purbeck marble, and ceiling paintings by the sixteenth-century artist, Lambert Barnard, which are

A view from Goodwood Racecourse towards Chichester and the sea

amongst the earliest attributable ones in the country.

Lewes and Chichester are as important now as they were centuries ago and have managed to grow in a civilized manner, retaining their sense of scale. Arundel, which for long ranked with them, has taken a different direction. Its setting on the slope of the Downs is reminiscent of Lewes, but unlike the latter, Arundel has, if anything, diminished in size over the last 100 years. It is dominated by two buildings, both of which happen to belong essentially to the late nineteenth century, a period otherwise virtually unrepresented in the architecture of the town. One is the castle, the other the cathedral of St Philip Neri. Although the former goes back to before the Norman Conquest, what was left of it in the 1890s was so extensively rebuilt that it must rank as Victorian. The cathedral is built in the French Gothic style and as the castle is mock-medieval both give the appearance of being much older than they are and might at first glance seem to be amongst the most venerable instead of almost the newest.

Arundel does not seem particularly small when one is standing in the middle of its main street beneath the castle walls, but it has no suburbs and its population, 2,500, is hardly more than that of a large village. Traffic congestion is no problem, thank goodness, a newly completed system of ring roads ensuring that only those vehicles which have business in the town need enter it. Arundel Castle, the home of the Earl Marshal of England, the Duke of Nor-folk, is best seen from a distance, when the clumsiness of its Victorian rebuilding hardly shows and the impressive effect of its outline, whether against the Downs or the sky-line, is what counts.

St Philip Neri, the cathedral church of the Roman Catholic Bishop of Arundel and Brighton, provides an effective foil to the castle but it can also stand closer scrutiny. Delicately proportioned and with a lovely spire, it has an air of elegance which looks well from any angle, whether glimpsed from within the town down side turnings or over rooftops or in its entirety from a distance. I once attended Mass there on a June evening the day after the wedding of the daughter of the late Duke of Norfolk, when all the decorations for the great day were still in evidence, including a bouquet of white lilies at the end of each pew, and the cool and peace after the congestion of the roads and the excessive heat of Climping Beach where my family and I had spent the afternoon was such as would surely have occasioned the most devout atheist a moment's reflection. Unfortunately the serenity was short-lived; our smallest son kicked up such a racket we had to leave before the service was half over.

It is generally believed that King Alfred had the first castle at Arundel erected on a site overlooking the Arun, at that time the only practical route from the sea to the Weald between the Hampshire border and Shoreham, Stane Street having fallen largely into disuse. William the

Arundel

Conqueror gave Arundel and its title to Roger Montgomery, who had accompanied him at Hastings, and the Norman arch and walls still stand. In 1580 the castle passed to Thomas Howard, fourth Duke of Norfolk, Earl of Surrey and Earl Marshal of England. He chose to back Mary Queen of Scots against Elizabeth and lost his head as a consequence. His son Philip refused to give up his allegiance to Rome and he too was sentenced to death. The sentence was not carried out but he died after eleven years of suffering in the Tower of London. The castle then became Elizabeth's property, was restored to the Howard family by James I, and apart from being held by the Parliamentarians for a time during the Civil War, has remained with them ever since. Cromwell's troops reduced much of the building to ruins and although some restoration was carried out in the eighteenth century, it is the late Victorian rebuilding which predominates.

The late Duke (the sixteenth), the thirty-seventh Earl of Arundel, was a great cricket enthusiast. Each touring team would play a one-day match against an invitation team of the Duke's at Arundel, he was president of the M.C.C., and manager of an M.C.C. side in Australia. His interest and involvement in the game at local, county and national level is reflected throughout Sussex and it is probably true to say that cricket has held an appeal in the county longer and more steadfastly than anywhere else in England.

The earliest reference to cricket so far discovered is of a game in Guildford in the sixteenth century; the second oldest concerns the parish of Boxgrove when, in 1622, it was alleged that some men of the village playing in the churchyard on a Sunday did "cause to breake the church windows with the ball . . . that a little childe had like to have her braynes beaten out with a cricket batt". The grip the game had on Boxgrove was such that even the churchwardens were accused of "defending and mayntayning" the cricketers. By the end of the seventeenth century the game had become extremely popular although H. F. and A. P. Squire in their *Pre-Victorian Sussex Cricket* suggest that its origins go back into pre-history and that cricket as we know it is "an emasculated form of murderous strife". Certainly poor Henry Brand of Selsey found it murderous enough, for in 1647 he was hit on the head by a bat and killed. The first record of an organized match anywhere in the country occurs at Dicker in 1677, and soon newspapers were reporting matches in Sussex and the neighbouring counties of Kent, Surrey, Hampshire and London. It has been suggested that the grip of Puritanism on the capital and the towns caused the young dogs of the time to search elsewhere for their pleasures and thus they discovered the game. They formalized the rules and introduced gambling on an enormous scale. In 1747 a women's match involving participants from four Sussex villages attracted "the greatest number of spectators of both sexes ever seen at any public diversion" and the gambling at a match between

Brighton and the M.C.C. in 1792 reached such a pitch that personal items, including watches and jewellery, were wagered.

The first recorded cricketer out of a long and continuing line of great Sussex players was Richard Newland of Slindon, who practised as a surgeon in Chichester in the latter part of the eighteenth century. Then there was William Lillywhite who first played in Goodwood Park in 1822. He introduced round-arm bowling and thirty-two years later at the age of sixty-one was still playing for England.

In the early days any team, not always of eleven players, could call itself the county—or, indeed, England—team, and it wasn't until 1839 that the Sussex County Club was formed; it moved to its present headquarters at Hove in 1872, although county matches are played elsewhere in Sussex; at Horsham, Hastings, Eastbourne and Worthing. Another member of the Lillywhite family, James, was the first captain of an England team to tour Australia, in 1876–7. Two test matches were played, England losing the first and winning the second. From the age of twenty James Lillywhite played for the Sussex team without a break for twenty years and then umpired for another twenty. In the last match the Sussex team ever played against England, John Wisden, founder of the celebrated almanac, helped his side to victory by taking eight England wickets for forty-one runs.

Cricket on the edge of the Downs at Findon

Although the county side and its illustrious members naturally attracted the greatest attention, the real strength of the game lay in the village sides which flourished on grounds good, bad and indifferent. There were a number of pitches up on the level parts of the Downs which must have bred an especially agile race of deep fieldsmen.

89

The game is hardly less popular today. A match in progress on a picturesque Sussex village green, perhaps with the Downs in the background—at Burpham for example, or East Dean, Ditchling or Ringmer—is for many people a symbol of England; whilst throughout the present century the county team has provided the national side with a succession of gifted players, ranging from the graceful Indians, Ranjisinghi, and Daleepsinghi; that tireless bowler Maurice Tate; the long-serving Langridge brothers; Jim Parks, a fine wicketkeeper-batsman and son of another famous county player; to the fiery John Snow and two outstanding all-rounders, Ted Dexter and Tony Greig—Dexter and Greig being captains of both county and country. It was a nice touch that an adopted Sussex man should captain England in that marvellous commemorative Test at Melbourne in March 1977, Tony Greig emulating James Lillywhite's achievement of 100 years earlier.

CHAPTER SIX

Eastwards to Pulborough, Steyning and Burgess Hill

The inland route from Arundel eastwards will take us first of all north through the woods, up the steep hill beside the castle grounds, to where the Bognor and Littlehampton roads converge at the top of Bury Hill, with glorious views over the Arun valley and the Downs. Some of the most attractive villages in Sussex are within walking distance of Bury Hill: Bury itself, Amberley, Burpham, West Burton, Sutton and Bignor. It is not surprising that artists and writers have chosen to live here. The house in Bury which Galsworthy had built and where he wrote much of *The Forsyte Saga* can be clearly seen from the hill, and nearer still, down the B2139 road to Storrington, just before it crosses the Arun, is Houghton House where the greatest of English illustrators, Arthur Rackham, lived from 1920 to 1929. Both Galsworthy and Rackham used the Sussex landscape in their work; Chanctonbury Ring, for example, provides the setting for a famous scene between Jon and Fleur in *The Forsyte Saga*, whilst the river scenes in Rackham's illustrations for *The Vicar of Wakefield* and *The Compleat Angler*, amongst others, must surely be along the Arun.

Amberley, just across the river from Houghton and once linked to Bury by ferry, has many times been called the most beautiful village in Sussex, and therefore, perhaps, in England. Its thatched cottages and houses; its twelfth-century church, built on the site of a wooden one erected by St Wilfrid; its castle, once home of the bishops of Chichester; and its superb setting between the Downs and the Arun; these have all been painted many times. Indeed, its features were at one time as familiar at the Royal Academy as those of certain captains of industry and the Royal Family.

The next station up the line from Amberley is Pulborough. It is a pleasant seven-minute ride through the water meadows of the Arun; within sight of Amberley the train passes the site of Hardham Junction whence the line to Fittleworth, Petworth and Midhurst used to diverge. Perhaps the traffic problem in Petworth would not be quite so bad if it was still open, although it has to be said that the station was inconveniently far from the town. The track bed for part of its length now makes a fine, if sometimes overgrown, walk. Hardham has a tiny little church with some remarkable and almost unique twelfth-century murals, re-discovered quite by accident during the last century.

The abandoned Fittleworth Station on the Pulborough—Midhurst branch

Pulborough almost certainly owes its existence to the fact that it was a crossing place of the Arun, and the river has shaped the town and still dominates it. At this point it flows from west to east and the town centre is immediately north of it; at no point has it encroached beyond so that the often-flooded water meadows extend along the entire southern edge of Pulborough. Quite large pleasure boats sail up to the town, although nothing can get much further, owing to the famous seven-arch Stopham bridge a mile upstream. This early fifteenth-century structure, a replacement for an earlier wooden one, is typical, and considered by many to be the best, of a number of such bridges spanning the Arun and the western part of the Rother. It is in an idyllic setting with an old pub at the Pulborough side, the road disappearing up a hill deep in the trees at the other. It must surely have been the Arun around Stopham that Arthur Rackham had in mind for his last series of illustrations, those for *Wind in the Willows*, and there could be no more appropriate place to come across Mole, Ratty, Toad and all their river-bank companions. How splendid the yellow caravan would look coming up over the bridge! Although I am not sure Mr Toad would take very kindly to the signals which regulate the single line of traffic across it.

The road is the busy A283 between Guildford and Shoreham, but the bridge is not the bottleneck one might expect, except on the odd occasion. The preservation

The bridge at Stopham

order on it must certainly ensure its survival and should it ever be by-passed one hopes no one would ever be so insensitive as to build another alongside it and thus completely ruin both setting and bridge.

Stane Street passes through the middle of Pulborough and from Hardham (where it connected with the Greensand Way from Barcombe Mills) the Roman road is still in use as the A29 for twelve miles almost to the Surrey border. Stane Street's construction must have astonished the Britons and convinced them more comprehensively than any show of military force that resistance to Roman rule was futile. What must they have thought of the extraordinary men who appeared with sticks, held them up on tops of hills, signalled to each other, lit beacons at night, and then proceeded to organize them (the Britons) to build enormous embankments several feet high and up to thirty feet across, to put down a surface of gravel, the smoothness of which they had never before seen, and lo, there was a road, perfectly straight for mile after mile with only the occasional deviation, leading on, for all they knew, to the end of the world.

Ivan D. Margary, who lived at Hartfield until his death in 1976, is the authority on Roman roads in England. His book, *Roman Ways in the Weald*, revives and increases one's admiration of the extraordinary engineering and civilizing skills of the people who ruled Britain for 400 years, for their communications system made almost everything possible. If only the Dark Ages which followed the end of the Roman Empire had been avoided, where might civilization have been now?

However, we are still at Pulborough and it might be worth noting that 160 years ago before the coming of either the railway—which arrived from London in 1859—or the revival of Stane Street after the introduction of the motor car, the town stood on another through route between the capital and the coast. This was a water-way which used the River Wey (which joins the Thames at Chertsey) and the River Arun with a canal between them, and the canalization of sections of both where this was necessary, including some locks. Quite a lot of this sort of work was carried out on and adjacent to Sussex rivers in the early decades of this century, but it was barely complete before the railway arrived and put an end to the traffic, which, for a short time was quite substantial.

The last development of this kind was along the Adur in 1826, and during the 1830s, 115 miles of canal or canalized river flourished in Sussex, but by the end of that decade work had started on the Brighton line. Barge traffic between the coast and London ceased passing through Pulborough in 1868, the same year the upper reaches of the Ouse ceased commercial operation. The Adur canalization was abandoned in 1875, the western Rother in 1880, and finally in 1888 barges ceased to penetrate the upper reaches of the Arun above Pulborough. In some cases

94

The London–Bognor road at Pulborough

there was a legal abandonment, in others the powers were just let go. Remnants of some of the old locks may still be found, as may a stretch of the canal built alongside the Arun between Billingshurst and Wisborough Green. Barges used some of the lower stretches of the rivers until the Second World War, but no commercial water-borne traffic penetrates further into Sussex than the harbours at the estuaries of the Arun, the Adur, the Ouse and the eastern Rother today.

Pulborough once had a castle, probably built after the Norman Conquest, of which little more is known than its site, some distance to the north-west of the town; and a manor house which probably stood where the fifteenth-century New Place now is. The parish church of St Mary at the top of the short wooded hill, up which the A29 climbs from the crossroads by the river, is very handsome, and dates mostly from the early fifteenth century. Opposite is an extraordinary old half-timbered house, built out of the rock of the cutting, through which the main-road traffic thunders.

Storrington, where the Pulborough and Amberley roads converge, has grown considerably in the last 100 years. Like Pulborough, it probably has its origins as a crossing place, in this case of the Stor, a stream which rises in the Downs and joins the Arun at Pulborough. It was a market town in 1399 and possessed a church and two mills at the time the *Domesday Book* was written. The oldest part of the parish church of St Mary the Virgin is the nave, which is early Norman, although there was much restoration in Victorian times and in the 1920s. The West Sussex Gold Club was opened at Storrington in 1930 and, should this have failed to provide sufficient diversion, a guide book of the period noted that in the village hall was "a library of over 2,000 volumes and a wireless".

The most distinguished building in the vicinity is Parham, an Elizabethan manor house, a mile and a half to the west of Storrington, beautifully landscaped in 350 acres against the Downs. Elizabeth I visited Parham in 1591 and is said to have sat under one of the famous oak trees, ever afterwards known as 'Betsy's Oak'.

Storrington belongs to a group of ancient inland towns set immediately north of the Downs, which since the last century have been rather overshadowed by the new resorts by the sea. Before we reach the next, Steyning, the road passes the fine, old, and now quiet, village of Washington, above which is the best known landmark on the Downs, the 814-foot-high Chanctonbury Ring. It is a hill fort, probably of Neolithic origin, although in use during Roman times, and now crowned by a circle of beeches planted in 1760 by Charles Goring who lived at Wiston, an Elizabethan house like Parham, a mile away at the foot of the Downs.

Seven miles east of Storrington are the twins; Steyning and Bramber. I have elsewhere defined Bramber as a

Washington, with Chanctonbury in the background

The view across the Adur from the ramparts of Bramber Castle

village and Steyning as a town, principally on the grounds that the latter, with a population of around 4,000, is the larger, but both were important places 1,000 years ago.

One of the first acts of King William after the Conquest was to set up a form of administration in Sussex which would ensure that good order prevailed throughout the county, an essential precaution to preserve communications with Normandy. He therefore divided the county into *rapes* (a word deriving from the old Icelandic word for rope, marking a division), these being Hastings, Pevensey, Lewes, Bramber, Arundel and Chichester. Bramber was chosen because of its position beside the Adur, and the castle is thought to have been built by William de Braose, feudal lord of Bramber, in the years immediately after the Conquest. What remains of it stands on a hill high over the village overlooking the parish church.

The river divided Steyning and Bramber and the port was situated at the former. Sea-going craft used it in Saxon times and continued to do so into the twelfth century, but by that time silting caused William de Braose to build a new harbour on the other side of the Downs, much nearer the sea at New Shoreham. Sometime shortly after this Steyning Harbour fell into disuse and now not even its site is known, although it has been suggested that it was at the end of a bay immediately north of the parish church of St Andrew, a mile from where the river now flows.

St Andrew's is a particularly fine church of the late Norman period. There was a church here before this in the eighth century, and Ethelwulf, father of King Alfred, was buried at Steyning. Steyning owes its existence to that curious saint, Cuthnan, who is said to have wheeled his aged mother in a barrow when they went on their travels. This vehicle eventually became unroadworthy at Steyning, Cuthnan took this as a sign from heaven and settled on the spot, building a wooden church.

A good deal of the medieval town survives, including the old Market House, and it was designated a Conservation Area in 1973. In the early 1930s a preservation society was set up in order to keep a watchful eye on development and the incursion of motor traffic, and one of its first successes was the removal of some advertisement hoardings. It also succeeded in persuading shopkeepers to retain their original small windows and to use well-designed, unobtrusive signs to maintain the character of the town. Steyning had a station on the Brighton to Horsham branchline until 1966, which helped to keep some traffic out of the narrow main street; there are also plans for a by-pass to the north-east.

Steyning was once famous for its ox fair. Oxen tend to have a medieval, or even biblical connotation, but in fact they were common on the Sussex Downs until the end of the last century. A team usually consisted of six animals, working in pairs, although in earlier days they had been

99

Team of Sussex oxen at Exceat in 1923

in the winter and grass in the summer. An ox was steadier than a horse and needed no grooming, and these qualities, together with the beneficial effects of cloven hoofs on chalky soil, ensured his survival on the Sussex Downs into modern times. He was broken into the plough at $2\frac{1}{2}$ years old, worked for five years and then was pensioned off, not to a life of ease but to the butcher. The First World War virtually ended his career; beef prices went so high that it paid farmers still using ox teams to send them to the slaughterhouse whether or not there was any work left in them.

There were other factors in the decline of the ox, and Maude Robinson in her account of life on a farm in the latter part of the nineteenth century wrote, "the real reason that oxen were given up as draught animals was that they made too unwieldly a team to draw that blessed invention, the self-binding reaper, and the younger workmen disliked their slow pace". The latter is probably the key both to the ox team's longevity and its eventual disappearance.

The small farmer has always been a conservative fellow. To us today a nineteenth-century ox team plodding steadily across the Downs symbolizes the unchanging traditions of rural England, an image for a pre-Raphaelite painter turning his back on the steam train belching smoke as it rushes across the Ouse Viaduct towards Brighton with its party of day-trippers. It is a romantic notion, but we may

used in line. They were at their most popular at the end of the eighteenth century, the Sussex Red, which was often crossed with Welsh or Hereford cattle, being considered the best breed in the kingdom. Horses were faster and more intelligent, although an ox was not as stupid as is commonly supposed, and was stronger. He was also a less fussy eater than a horse, being content with hay and straw

be grateful we are not the small farmer who owned that ox team; for his lack of education, his fear of change, his poverty and his incomprehension of the benefits mechanization could bring to the land condemned him to a life of hard, monotonous work for little reward, scarcely more congenial than that of those who laboured in the mills and mines of the Midlands and the North. The very last ox team in Sussex worked at Birling Manor, near Exceat; the names of the oxen were Lump, Leader, Pilot, Pedlar, Quick and Nimble. In 1928 they went into retirement on the Pevensey Marshes and eventually, perhaps sadly, perhaps fittingly, were sold for beef. They were not quite the end of the story, for ox teams may still be seen at shows in Sussex, particularly at the South of England Show at Ardingly.

The next station up the now-vanished railway line, four miles north of Steyning, is Henfield. In the early 1960s it was still described as a village, but it is surely a town, with its long main street on the A281 Horsham to Brighton road and the development to the west of this. The parish church of St Peter dates back to the thirteenth century, but was much restored in the nineteenth. Henfield is an attractive place with a fair number of interesting old houses, close enough to Brighton to be within easy commuting distance but large enough and sufficiently distant to have a life of its own.

Very much more a product of the railway age and dependent upon Brighton are three still-expanding towns and their satellites, centred upon the stations at Haywards Heath, Wivelsfield, Burgess Hill and Hassocks.

The arrival of the railway at Haywards Heath in 1841 began a process of expansion which has continued from then until now. In 1800 there were eight farmhouses, nine cottages, two inns and a windmill, forming a scattered rural community set between the ancient market towns of Cuckfield and Lindfield, and the station was built primarily to serve these two towns. In 1861 an Act of Parliament put an end to the long-standing common rights, twelve plots were sold off as building land and the development began. A substantial church, St Wilfrid's, was built in 1863, in yellow stone and red tiles, overlooking what had become the park; a cattle-market was established in 1867, and by virtue of the growing rail system, which by the end of the century directly linked Haywards Heath not only with places up and down the London to Brighton line, but with Lewes, Newhaven, Eastbourne, Horsted Keynes, East Grinstead and beyond, it became the largest in central Sussex. At the turn of the century the population numbered 2,500 people, 400 of whom were school children; there was a county court, a lunatic asylum, and, from 1894 onwards, a Haywards Heath Urban District Council.

Three miles to the south, Burgess Hill grew in an identical manner, beginning with a common enclosure in 1828 and speeding up with the opening of its station thirteen

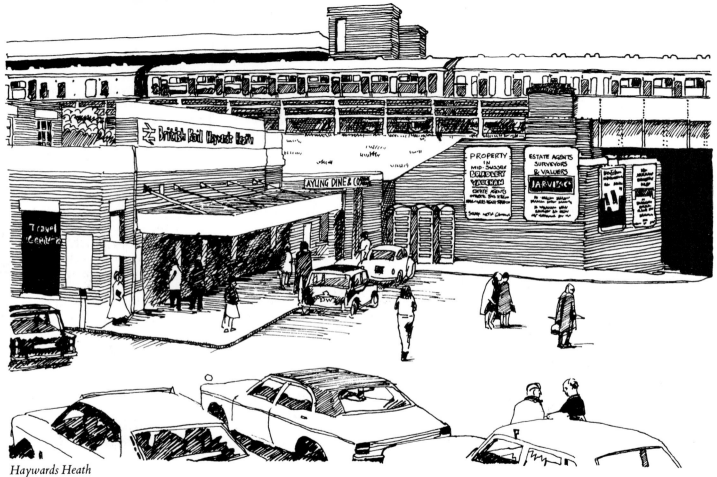

Haywards Heath

years later. It too achieved the status of an Urban District in 1894. Its parish church, St John the Evangelist, was completed two years before the one at Haywards Heath and is a good deal more distinguished. Constructed primarily of red brick, a material which Victorian church architects did not, on the whole, use with much aplomb, it is inlaid with courses of blue-grey bricks which create a pleasing decorative effect. St John's possesses a handsome, tiled spire, and the ornate brick wall surrounding the churchyard enhances the general effect and sense of careful attention which the architect, T. Talbot Bury, achieved.

Burgess Hill's first industry, and one which still exists, was that of brick and tile making. Church Road, linking the church with the station, rapidly became the town's principal shopping street. Recently the western half, nearest the church, has become a pedestrian precinct. Beside it has been built a large shopping and community centre (Martlet's Hall) a library, and a multi-storey car park, all in brick of a similar shade to that of the church opposite and thus continuing the sense of good design. There is less evidence of concern for any visual relationship with its neighbours when it comes to Sussex House, the large four-storey office block opposite, although it is nicely landscaped into the extensive lawns which border the new Civic Way linking Church and Station Roads.

Burgess Hill has spread out in all directions from its original centre around the church and the station, particularly to the west, across the A273 Haywards Heath to Brighton road, where the industrial centre is, and northwards, embracing Wivelsfield Station, one mile away, and perilously close to the southern fringes of Haywards Heath. Burgess Hill's greatest period of growth was between 1951 and 1961 when the population rose by 64 per cent. In that decade it was, apart from the New Towns, the fastest growing town in the South-East, and the population now numbers 20,000.

Had the ribbon development of the 1920s and '30s gone on unchecked, there is little doubt that the entire area bordering the Brighton line from the Surrey border to the sea would by now be built up. Planning restrictions prevented this, nevertheless there is not much open country in the eight-mile stretch from Lindfield to Hassocks, just a small area between Haywards Heath and Burgess Hill and another one between the latter and the Keymer–Hassocks–Hurstpierpoint conglomeration.

The Strategic Plan for the South-East, published in 1970, did not hold out much hope of even this lasting very long. Sensible, sympathetic planning is essential and has done much to preserve the Sussex countryside and coast in the last forty years, but the 1970 Strategic Plan was not, perhaps, one of its more shining achievements. There is a distinctly sinister Orwellian touch about its designation of that part of Sussex boarded by Crawley and Burgess Hill as "Planning Area Six" and its "call for an early sub-

The Parish Church of St John the Evangelist, Burgess Hill

Burgess Hill, from the churchyard

PETER HOLLING DALE

regional appraisal to indicate whether provision can be made for a total population of over 450,000 . . . by the end of the century" is enough to give anyone the shivers. In the event, the unexpected decline in the birthrate and the financial recession have combined, fortuitously in this instance, to reverse trends and bring to a halt developments which seemed inevitable a decade ago.

Because Haywards Heath and Burgess Hill are neither very old nor very beautiful and are surrounded by places which are, writers and visitors tend to look down upon them, at worst dismissing them as blots upon the landscape, at best grudgingly admitting them to be convenient centres from which to mount expeditions to centres of greater historical, cultural and visual appeal. But this ignores the all-important fact that towns and villages are primarily for living and working in, and that the enormous growth of Haywards Heath and Burgess Hill must surely suggest that an awful lot of people have found conditions there very much more congenial than in many apparently more attractive places.

A modern, not very large but skilfully designed house, wasting not an inch of space, centrally heated, labour-saving, on an estate full of similar homes, precisely fits the requirements of a great many young married couples. They will be living amongst people of their own kind, their children will grow up surrounded by their friends, they will form community associations and baby-sitting circles; they will join sports clubs, amateur dramatic societies, Oxfam, Amnesty International, the Save the Children Fund, the P.T.A.; they will make great use of, for example, the Dolphin Leisure Centre at Haywards Heath, with its swimming pools, gym, squash courts, sauna and solarium, or the similar Martlet's Hall at Burgess Hill; they will find the health centre, the library, the supermarkets and shopping centres greatly convenient—a car for getting out into the country or the seaside is a necessity, although almost equally necessary is a nearby main-line station for getting to work at Brighton, Crawley, Croydon or London. They will almost certainly not belong to a wife-swapping group, the National Front or the Trotsky-ites; very possibly they will have been born and raised outside Sussex, quite possibly in Scotland, Wales or Ireland, but not in India, Pakistan or the West Indies; they pay their taxes and rates, hope their children will get into the 'O' level stream at the comprehensive, and they care about their community.

Their "little boxes" are an easy target, especially for those who can afford something grander and for those free-wheelers who have opted out of commitments to nine-to-five employment, a mortgage and a family; an option society has made possible chiefly because it is financed and guaranteed by the inhabitants of the little boxes, just as these inhabitants would in turn find it unthinkable that the church, whether Church of England, Nonconformist or Roman Catholic, should ever close its doors to them, although only a fairly small proportion ever passes beyond them. The apparent all-pervading conformity of a community such as that of Haywards Heath or Burgess Hill is, of course, an illusion. Shared aims, common—if unstated—standards in no way necessitate a subjugation of personality. Within every little box live individuals, each with his or her own unique ancestry, background, values and aspirations. I am sure there are as many eccentrics, improbable ambitions, unfulfilled desires, horrific propensities, aspirations to saintliness and staggering potentialities within six miles of the Mid-Sussex District Council offices in Boltro Road, Haywards Heath, as in almost any other inhabited part of the universe.

Not very many towns are celebrated in music, but Donald Swann once wrote a song, part comical, part affectionate, called "God Bless the Community of Haywards Heath". The young assistant in the library at Haywards Heath told me in a somewhat taken aback tone, "There isn't enough to the place", when I asked her if anyone had ever written a history of it, but I do not believe her. Enough goes on every day to fill a book, and a good deal of it could be gathered simply by listening to other people's conversations. Just one illustration, overheard in a local health centre, must suffice. One lady was telling her friend about some sardine sandwiches she had made for her lorry-driver husband. She had given the remaining contents of the tin to the cat for its breakfast and was horrified to notice an hour or so later that the animal was staggering around with a glazed expression in its eyes. Assuming that something was wrong with the fish, she telephoned her husband's employers, only to be told he had already left the yard and was driving up the motorway. The police were contacted and they traced him, took him to hospital, had his stomach pumped out and found nothing wrong. The next morning the milkman knocked on the lady's door and asked if the cat was all right. She replied that he had been ill but was better and why was the milkman asking? "Well," he said, "yesterday I dropped a bottle of milk on his head."

Uckfield is best known for its traffic-jams, which reach epic proportions at weekends in high summer. I have never quite been able to account for them. Certainly there is a level-crossing in the centre of the town, but its gates are open only for a couple of minutes in each hour, and its effect on the traffic flow, or lack of it, is minimal. The A22 London to Eastbourne and the A26 Maidstone to Brighton roads come together at the north end of the town and diverge at the southern end, but the congestion extends both before and beyond their junctions; there is no obvious bottleneck in the town centre and one can only conclude that there exists a perverse law of traffic flow which decrees that weekend motorists will automatically create a jam whatever the conditions. There is no obvious

Uckfield from the south

108

alternative route although, as with any other country town, if one knows the area well enough one can find one's way around through the surrounding lanes.

The oldest part of Uckfield is at the top of the steep main street, the newest being a huge housing estate to the north-west, built on land which belonged to the Nevill family and adjoining Buxted Park. A large proportion of Uckfield's population of around 5,000 lives on this estate which was completed seven years ago. Buxted, a village with a church built within the park, now plays second fiddle to Uckfield but it was once much more important. It was a centre of the iron industry and the first mention of Uckfield, in a document dated 1291, refers to the parish of "Buxted cum Uckfield". Until the fourteenth century the parish church of Holy Cross, Uckfield, was a chapel-of-ease to Buxted. The present church is largely Victorian, although it looks much older, and stands at the centre of the oldest and most attractive part of the town. Round the corner from Church Street in the main road is the Maiden's Head, a Georgian inn which was an important staging post in coaching days. On the corner itself are the remains of what must once have been a rather grand mansion. These consist of some passages and a vaulted stone room incorporated into more modern buildings.

Just what form the mansion took and to whom it belonged is a mystery. Uckfield has remarkably little written history and in the *Historic Towns of Sussex*, prepared by the Institute of Archaeology, University of London, for the Department of the Environment, and published in 1976, the town is not mentioned, presumably because there has been a negligible amount of research done on it. There is no guide to the church and practically nothing of local interest in the library. Odd fragments of the past survive, one of the more esoteric being that a certain Arnold bought eighty-two gallons of beer with which to entertain Edward I when he stayed in Uckfield, perhaps in the mysterious mansion, on 23rd June 1299.

A bit further down the High Street from its junction with Church Street is a cinema which has managed to stay open. Beyond is the main shopping area, consisting of some undistinguished twentieth-century architecture, and at the bottom of the hill the bus and railway stations and the river, officially anonymous but known locally and logically as the Uck.

Past the river and the level-crossing the road climbs as steeply as it descends through what used to be known as New Uckfield by way of the police station, the Victoria Pleasure Gardens, some large late nineteenth-century houses and the Roman Catholic Church of Our Lady Immaculate of St Philip Neri. Consecrated in 1963, this church attracted a good deal of attention in religious and architectural circles and the designs for the glasswork were hung in the Royal Academy. Much devotion and care was put into its design and construction. The parish priest, Cyril Plummer, wrote in 1963,

> Whether or not the work has been successful is not for the writer to judge, but it would be very ungracious to ignore the remarks of the many hundreds of visitors who have come here, to the effect that the church has a spiritual atmosphere about it; it seems to have a spirit of prayer.

As one who has worshipped in it on many occasions, whilst in no way detracting from the vigorous spiritual and social life of which it is a centre, it does not seem to me to have quite come off. As in many modern churches, there are too many diverse notions and intentions in conflict in the fittings, the furnishings and the decorations and the devotional objects, and the result is an uneasy lack of calm and unawareness of the things of this world.

Heathfield, like Buxted, has a long and celebrated history of iron-making. For several generations the Fullers, who lived at Waldron two and a half miles south-west of what is now the town centre, were the ironmasters, and two of their guns, bearing the initials J. F., can be seen at the Tower of London. Heathfield guns often went all over the world with the British army and navy; they were used at the Siege of Gibraltar where the defending General George Elliot won himself the title Lord Heathfield. The furnace shut down in 1787 and Heathfield became a little-visited backwater immediately south of the ancient ridge-way linking Etchingham, Burwash and Uckfield, until,

nearly 100 years later, the railway arrived. It was only a single-track branchline and it has now gone but the changes it brought were many and permanent. They may not have been on the scale of those at Haywards Heath or Burgess Hill but they nevertheless brought New Heathfield into existence, leaving the original scattered village community around the church two miles away.

To this day there is a considerable tract of countryside between the town, with its population of around 4,000, and its parish church, All Saints. There are a number of nurseries in the district. In the early 1960s I spent two summers working at Victoria Station and one of my jobs was to unload boxes of carnations and chrysanthemums which arrived in the late afternoon from the Heathfield line. The flowers had to be got across London quickly in order to catch a northbound train at Kings Cross, ready for sale first thing the next morning. The Heathfield train's arrival coincided with the evening rush-hour and I fear we student porters were not over solicitous for the commuters' welfare as boxes of prize blooms hurtled around them out of the train and into the waiting road vans. Nowadays the railway plays no part in their travels, at least at the Sussex end. Other local industries include seed merchandizing, chicken rearing and processing at Buxted, and wine-making at Horam, two miles south of Heathfield. These two latter industries are very large and Buxted chickens and Merrydown wines are household names.

A view from Hurstpierpoint towards the South Downs

There was one other development in Heathfield's recent history which might have had a more revolutionary effect than all the others, although in the event it came to very little. This was the discovery of natural gas in 1895. A company was set up and announced its intention of supplying Brighton and Eastbourne, but it failed. However, the gas was used for research purposes for a time and for over thirty years illuminated the station.

Heathfield, despite its occasional forays into prominence, remains one of the lesser-known Sussex towns. Unlike its neighbours, Uckfield and Hailsham, it does not lie on or close to any of the busiest trunk routes and there has been little increase in the population since 1945. Most of its buildings date from the late nineteenth century and early twentieth century. With the railway gone and its bus services a pale shadow of what they once were it is not easily accessible other than by car. The shops serve the needs of the community and there is a weekly market. Essentially it is a town rooted, as it always has been, in the rich Wealden countryside.

CHAPTER SEVEN

Lewes, Hailsham and the Pevensey Marshes

No town in Sussex enjoys a finer setting than Lewes. Like Rye, Arundel and Petworth it stands on a hillside, but unlike them it continued to grow throughout the nineteenth century and into the twentieth. The railway had a good deal to do with this for unlike the other three, Lewes soon became an important junction. Its once busy goods and cattle yards have gone, as have two of its lines, but the remaining four flourish.

Lewes's continuing expansion has been both a blessing and an inconvenience. Its proximity to Brighton might have reduced it to the status of Steyning or Bramber, but it has survived and prospered. The price it has had to pay is an ever-increasing traffic problem, which did not begin to ease until the new river bridge was opened, and will not be overcome until the Southern Ring Road is completed.

Lewes derives its name from the Old English *hlaew*, which means a hill. It probably dates from around the time of Alfred, although the Caburn, an outcrop of the Downs immediately to the east, was occupied from the earliest times, being abandoned during the Roman era. Lewes prospered greatly after the Norman Conquest. The rape of Lewes was established and given to one of William's favourites, William de Warenne, and he it was who built the castle, the substantial remains of which survive to the present time. An equally impressive but long-vanished building, the Cluniac Priory of St Pancras, was begun in 1077. The pope of that time belonged to the Cluniac order and de Warenne built a church which at its greatest extent was nearly 450 foot long. Its downfall was dramatic. After the Dissolution of the Monasteries it was demolished, much of its stone being used in new construction work in various parts of the town and in the surrounding villages, and so thorough was its razing that for a time its site was in doubt. Excavation near the railway line has revealed a good deal of information about it, and some fragments of masonry, including part of one of the towers can now be seen; the Lewes Archaeological Group are still digging on the site.

The Battle of Lewes, fought in 1264 between Henry III and Simon de Montfort, is scarcely less important than the Battle of Hastings, for the treaty which Henry, the loser, was forced to sign, is generally regarded as marking the beginning of parliamentary democracy. Fought on the Downs to the east of the town, where the prison now stands and above Offham chalk pits, it was a most bloody

One of the famous Brighton-built Atlantics passing through Lewes with the Newhaven Boat Train

battle, resulting in appalling bloodshed on both sides; pieces of metal and bone are still being recovered from the site.

Some 300 years later, when the country was again divided, during the brief restoration of the Roman Catholic faith by Queen Mary, Lewes was once more witness to violent death, this time in the heart of the town, in the High Street. Between 1555 and 1557 seventeen Sussex Protestants, including four women, were burned at the stake. Such was the revulsion these deaths aroused amongst ordinary people, particularly as within a year of the last burning Mary Tudor was dead and the Protestant Elizabeth was on the throne, that as late as the early years of the present century there was considerable antagonism to Roman Catholics, and when a Catholic church was being planned in Hailsham great difficulty was found in obtaining land for it.

Those who retained the Roman Catholic faith were much persecuted and their numbers dwindled throughout the sixteenth, seventeenth and eighteenth centuries, only reviving in the latter part of the nineteenth when more enlightened views began to prevail, coupled with the migration of many Irish families to the seaside towns. Today the Dublin, Kerry, Cork and Tipperary accents are often heard in Sussex pulpits and whilst the congregation of a country town parish has an unmistakably English look, that in one of the larger, older churches in Eastbourne or Brighton would not seem out of place in Limerick or a Dublin suburb, with worshippers standing in the aisles and many more children and young working class people in evidence than one finds at most Church of England services.

The last remnants of the anti-papist feelings, once so strong in Sussex, linger on in the annual Guy Fawkes celebrations held in Lewes, although they are now simply a riotous but innocent evening's entertainment. They began in the eighteenth century and by the 1820s had degenerated into little better than an excuse for wanton misbehaviour and vandalism. Flaming tar barrels and fire balls were let loose, mobs roamed the streets, shops and gratings were boarded up but were nevertheless in danger of being burned, and a magistrate was attacked outside his house. The climax was reached in 1847 when, despite the presence of a large force of police from London, the Riot Act had to be read from the steps of the County Hall. The mob still refused to disperse and was charged by the police, resulting in many injuries on both sides. For the next couple of years there was relative peace but an upsurge of anti-papist feeling around 1850 saw the setting up of a large bonfire close to the site of the execution of the Lewes Martyrs and the burning of effigies of the pope. In 1853 Bonfire Societies were formed, marches in fancy costume organized, and the whole affair gradually became a good deal more celebratory and jolly and

Lewes, a view to the south

much less malicious. It is largely in this form that it continues today, a measure of its widespread popularity and appeal being the great many children who attend, both as participants and spectators.

A nineteenth-century event which has passed into the folk-lore of the town took place on Christmas Eve, 1836. Snow fell so continuously and with such intensity that the town was cut off for three days, until the mail arrived, by foot, from East Grinstead. On the cliffs at the east end of the town a ridge of snow upwards of ten feet thick hung above South Street and Eastbourne Road. Some of this fell on a timber-yard on the evening of the 23rd with such force that it pushed it forty yards, and a number of the inhabitants of the adjacent Butchers Row were persuaded to leave their homes. Others, however, refused. Next morning it was apparent that these houses would be engulfed at any moment; two men dashed in, the occupants still would not budge, and the men just got clear as the snow crashed down. In the words of an eye-witness "not a vestige of habitation was to be seen—there was nothing but an enormous mound of pure white". Digging went on all day, despite a second fall, and eventually six people were recovered alive, and nine, chiefly women, were found dead.

Not all of Lewes's history, however, is violent, and in the year previous to the great snowstorm the Phoenix Ironworks was founded and contributed greatly to the town's prosperity in Victorian times and later. The first owner was John Every. To mark the firm's centenary, when it was still in the hands of the Every family, a number of seats were donated to Lewes and set up around the town, and a museum told the story of the by-now world-famous firm and its products, which were to be found in every continent. The tradition of Sussex iron still continues in Lewes and is commemorated in the new Phoenix bridge which crosses the Ouse beside the works and the industrial quarter of the town.

Lewes is a highly rewarding, if tiring town to walk around, its streets winding and twisting and swooping up and down in such a manner as to create a seemingly endless succession of vistas. In such a setting and amongst a generous spread of grass and trees even the least distinguished of buildings reveal qualities they would not possess elsewhere. In fact Lewes possesses many buildings of considerable distinction: the castle, Anne of Cleeves, house (now a folk museum), the Barbican House Museum, the Town Hall (formerly Star Inn), some splendid book shops and, in all, almost 200 Grade One and over 300 Grade Three structures.

The obvious, and best, starting-point for a tour of the town is the High Street. If we begin at the east end, under the cliffs, we at once become aware of the benefits of the new bridge, for the section of High Street east of the Ouse is now a quiet backwater instead of the trunk road of

High Street, Lewes

former days. The architecture in this section of the High Street, actually Cliffe High Street, Cliffe once being a suburb of Lewes, is a foretaste of much of what is to come, being predominantly Georgian. At the end is the rebuilt eighteenth-century bridge, with so pronounced a hump in its middle that one used almost instinctively to duck one's head to pass under the now demolished railway bridge which used to immediately follow it.

Beyond is a busy cross-roads and then up we go, climbing steeply past a mixture of Georgian and Victorian property to the centre of the town. To the left, at the bottom of the hill, are the station, the technical college, and the football ground. The college is large and modern and dull; the station is Victorian with lots of restored and imaginatively painted ironwork and decorative wooden awnings. Back on the top of the hill in the High Street are more Georgian shops and offices and some quite presentable twentieth-century imitations. The street narrows in the vicinity of the castle and here there are some very old buildings, including the fifteenth-century Bull Inn and a small fourteenth-century house.

The castle stands a short way to the north of the High Street, approached through a splendid fourteenth-century barbican. There is plenty of the castle left, including some of the original early Norman masonry, and one may climb to the top of the turrets. From there can be seen most of the town and a great deal of the countryside beyond, although curiously the castle is so placed that it cannot be seen from a large part of the town. The famous gaol and the Downs lie to the west, whilst to the south one may look along the valley of the Ouse past the tall chimney of the cement works at Beddingham towards Newhaven, although the Downs prevent a view of the sea. The most extensive view is to the north. The castle stands at the highest point for the best part of twenty miles and on a clear day one may look far beyond the water meadows alongside the Ouse as it winds towards Barcombe, over the Weald, past Uckfield, hidden in its valley, to the southern slopes of the Ashdown Forest beyond Buxted and to the Kent Border.

Glynde, set in a dip of the Downs three miles east of Lewes, is the birthplace of one of the most famous of Sussex exports, the Southdown sheep. It owes its pre-eminence to John Ellman, who lived at Glynde in the latter part of the eighteenth century and who spent his life breeding and developing the Southdown. Ellman's sheep, as he perfected it, and as it remains today, has a sturdy, compact air, with a thick carcass and a close, hard coat. Ellman's fleeces were the heaviest on the Downs, and although it was often considered that a light fleece produced the best wool, this was only true if the sheep was not looked after or carefully bred. Consequently Southdown fleeces gained the highest prices. Ellman sold his sheep all over the country, and soon they were being taken to the Colonies. Southdowns attained their greatest popularity in New Zealand, where today they are more plentiful than in this country, and in 1976 a gang of shearers came over from New Zealand to shear Sussex sheep.

It is perhaps more than a coincidence that one of the best known flocks of Southdowns grazes on the Downs just over the hill from Glynde, at Ringmer. It numbers between 300 and 400 and belongs to Mr John Craig, O.B.E., an astonishingly vigorous man of eighty-six. Mr Craig and his son are leading members of the Southdown Sheep Society, and maintain the breed's high standards, importing ewes from France and New Zealand and producing rams for cross-breeding on the Sussex and Kent marshes and elsewhere.

The best known book on Sussex Sheep is by Barclay Wills, published in 1930, full of information and anecdotes, but rather short on optimism, in that it sees the decline of sheep and shepherds, which had begun around the First World War, possibly continuing until the Southdown dies out. Having read the book I set out to find further, more up-to-date information, and did not make much headway for a time. The market at Hailsham was an almost complete washout, an auctioneer informing me that as far as he was concerned a sheep was "a pig with wool on it", and a shepherd, whilst perfectly willing to help, could only tell me about the cross-breeds he worked with on the flatter pastures of the Weald. However, my father happened to know a farmer, a Mr Walker, whose

Nelson Coppard (born in Poynings, 1863)

family had lived for generations at Looker's Cottage, out on the Pevensey Marshes; a looker is someone who looks after the sheep and cattle for a farmer or farmers who live some distance away.

Mr Walker told me that a looker usually had his own farm and land, and would go around once a day keeping an eye on all the sheep and cows in his care. He might also undertake to do the shearing and would present his bill to the farmer once a year in September. In a good year he might shear 1,000 sheep. The fleeces would be rolled up in packs weighing around half a ton and sent off from Hailsham Station to Chichester (nowadays they are collected by lorry and taken to Canterbury). When it was time for the sheep to leave the pastures on the marshes and go back to their own farms, which might be as far away as Uckfield or Heathfield, the looker would drive the flock halfway, say to Golden Cross if it was going to Uckfield, there they would take a rest and he would then hand over to the shepherd from Uckfield. It was Mr Walker who suggested I meet Mr Craig, and one bright, cold Sunday afternoon in January I went over to Ringmer to see him.

He told me that contrary to Barclay Wills's fears, the Southdown, although not as numerous in Sussex as it had once been, still flourished, and he pointed to the eastern slopes of the Caburn, a mile away, where his flock was grazing. The shepherd still stays out all night at lambing time, as he always has, although not in a hut out on the Downs with the sheep in pens for fear of foxes, but in the yard. Much dealing goes on at the annual Findon and Lewes Fairs, although the latter can hardly be the great event it was 100 years ago. Then Browne and Crosskey, of the High Street, would put out packing cases on the pavement so that people could sit on them whilst their friends and relations were trying on new clothes—an embroidered smock, possibly, perhaps a heavy white overcoat, fleecy outside lined with a cape, and maybe a billycock hat to protect the head when moving hurdles. Around the turn of the century the smock began to give way to "good corduroy suits and gaiters with a hard felt hat", but the traditional large umbrella lasted somewhile longer.

At night shepherds used horn lanterns, cylindrical with a cone on top. They were made by a Birmingham firm, which latterly replaced the dried, polished horn leaf with glass, which they confessed was "nothing like as good" and production ceased in 1915. Crooks are still used by shepherds, and still made in Sussex, at Pyecombe forge. Many are collectors' pieces, including a few brass ones. The first of these latter was made, as an experiment, at the L.B.S.C. Railway works at Brighton. It attracted a good deal of interest, and as a consequence others were made, but their use was limited for they broke easily. A shepherd, once he had found a crook of the right weight, was loth to part with it and might make a favourite one last thirty years, although it would by then be very worn.

Most old-time shepherds were content to spend all their lives out on the Downs with their sheep until they were deep into old age, and what thoughts they had up there on the bare, lonely slopes, and the flights of fancy the solitude encouraged, are largely unrecorded. But there are exceptions. John Dudeney in 1790, at the age of eight, started work as a shepherd boy helping his father near Lewes. His mother taught him to read, his father to add and subtract, and any money he could spare from the £6 a year he received on being promoted to the position of under-shepherd at the age of sixteen he spent on books. These he stored in a hole in the turf, which he covered with a stone, and such was the education he thus acquired that, in 1804, when he was twenty-two, he gave up his flock to become a teacher in Lewes.

Stephen Blackmore belonged to a later generation, being born in 1833. Despite losing his right arm in a threshing accident at the age of 17, he became one of the most celebrated of Downland shepherds. During his long life—he died in Steyning Workhouse in 1920 at the age of eighty-seven—he used his keen eyes to gather together what was described as "one of the finest private collections of flint implements in the country". Stephen Blackmore became almost a national figure. A grandson of his was named after the explorer, H. M. Stanley, whom Stephen particularly admired, and the Geological Society sent him the complete works of Stanley, whilst Charles Kingsley personally presented him with a copy of *The Water Babies*. In their old age he and his wife moved into the almshouses at Seaford but the latter died within a fortnight. She had been a beautiful young woman and a handsome old lady. Stephen wrote of her, "she was serviceable to the last of her life and died in Pease. I am lonely now. Bess so many years had been a good wife, my dear friend. It seems she did not suffer". Few people could ask for a better obituary.

Hailsham is set in the middle of the sheep-rearing district, with the Weald to the north, the Downs, immediately behind Beachy Head, to the south, and the Pevensey Marshes, or Levels, extending up to its borders. Like every town in Sussex it is unique, yet at the same time it may be said to be typical. Its history is long, and much of it may be discovered simply by walking about it with one's eyes open, but it has also developed and grown greatly in the twentieth century. It happens to be the Sussex town I know best, for I lived there for some years, and therefore I hope the reader will indulge my lingering over it a while.

Hailsham's great day is Wednesday, market day. Then most of the inhabitants of East Sussex—or so it sometimes seems, converge on the town. I have travelled on the mid-morning bus from Heathfield, which by the time it had half-completed its journey was packed like a Cairo tram with more than thirty people standing, and for the last part of the journey would-be passengers had to be left by the roadside all along the way. A few years earlier the now-abandoned railway, which our overladen vehicle crossed and re-crossed some half-dozen times, would have been happy to cope with the excess, but higher powers than the Hailsham Rural District Council decided it was not needed.

The market is held on a site near the town centre, south-east of the parish church, the tower of which—if one is fortunate enough to obtain permission to climb it—provides a fine vantage point from which to view the entire scene. The entrance is half-way along Market Street, behind a high brick wall. On the immediate right as one enters are stalls selling china, crockery, fabrics, haberdashery, toys, etc.; some of the stallholders being shopkeepers in the town, the majority coming from further afield. Opposite is the cattle market, a circular building, rather like a small permanent circus, with an open central ring and covered-in standing space and several tiers of benches all around. I suppose a visitor from Spain might momentarily think himself in a miniature bull-ring when the gate is thrown open and several hundred pounds of beef makes its appearance; he would almost immediately realize his mistake at the sight of the docile Sussex bullock. Outside are the pens for cattle awaiting their cue, and further on ones full of sheep and pigs. These latter present a somewhat gory appearance, with blood dripping from their ears where they have been marked by their new owners, all the while squealing and grunting, barging and nipping at each other, and generally giving a very fair imitation of a bad-tempered political demonstration caught up in the first day of the winter sales.

Elsewhere there are auctions of eggs, poultry and vegetables, but the sale which attracts the largest crowd is held at the northern extremity of the market. Here may be found anything from gramophone records to motor cars. Bicycles, washing machines, carpets, oil paintings, brass bedsteads, armchairs, bean sticks, tool kits, photograph albums and almost anything else which does not moo, bleat or cackle but which someone might find a use for is likely to turn up. As might be supposed it is a great place for bargains. On some occasions prices are astonishingly low, although one can never safely predict what something will fetch beforehand, for it all depends on how many potential buyers it has. Furniture prices, for instance, vary greatly and an apparently highly unprepossessing piece will attract a number of bidders, while one much easier on the eye might be knocked down for 50p. or 75p.

At noon the auctioneer emerges from his office, battles his way through to the first object, and the main event of the day is under way. There are likely to be more spectators than bidders; most of the regulars noting that children's bicycles are still much in demand, that a settee is back

Hailsham Market

for the third time within a couple of months, that whoever bought Beethoven's Ninth on a set of seventy-eights should have looked more closely beforehand, unless he preferred "The Laughing Policeman" to the middle of the Slow Movement, and that black and white televisions are not the favourites they once were. Of those who do bid a number are also regulars, dealers from Eastbourne, Lewes and elsewhere, but more are local people, housewives, farmworkers and the like on the lookout for a good kitchen chair, a serviceable mower or a child's pedal car.

Some of the best fun comes if an item has not been sold and the auctioneer lumps it in with the next one, so that whoever wants the picture frames gets landed with an additional boxful of tarnished cutlery. Every so often, when the group following the auctioneer merges with another group which has stood guard for twenty minutes over an item it intends to bid for, the crush becomes too much, there is an appeal for elbow room, and everyone grudgingly moves back a little. Wet days are best for bargain hunting, when the casual bidders are absent, and bed quilts and open boxes of assorted nuts and bolts do not show to their best advantage, but otherwise there is no closed season and there are as likely to be as many people about in winter as in summer.

Not so long ago it would have been true to say that the south-eastern extremity of the market marked the edge of the town. Now it is surrounded by houses and more and more are being built. Hailsham has grown at a great rate in the last few years, the population practically doubling in the ten years prior to 1971, and it is still climbing. It then numbered 10,138, having been 5,955 in 1961. Previous to that its growth had been slow and steady, there being 4,788 townspeople in 1951; 4,031 in 1931; 3,369 in 1891; 2,098 in 1861; and around 1,000 at the end of the eighteenth century.

The first recorded reference to the town is in the *Domesday Book*, when it was known as Hamelsham. The origins of the name, of which there have been many variations, can only be conjecture, apart from the certainty that they are Saxon, but they may have something to do with *haile*, which means safe, or possibly it was known as the settlement of *Hella*, *Heile* or some such Saxon. The oldest easily identifiable spot is the pond, now bordered by Station Road and Bell Banks Road, where the bells of the parish church were cast—and the gasworks. The pond certainly existed in 1263, when there is mention of an accidental drowning in it, and there is little doubt that it is as old as the town itself. It is a sizeable piece of water for a pond, with a small island in the centre, and is well looked after by the council who have it cleaned out every so often, which is the only time a boat is seen upon it. It is particularly popular, as no doubt it always has been, with swans and fishermen.

The oldest architecture in Hailsham is to be found in the

parish church where a small piece of the original twelfth-century building remains, although a flint wall in an alleyway off the Market Square is said to run it a close second. Much the most handsome building in the town is the former vicarage, a lovely red brick Queen Anne house.

The centre of Hailsham consists of a triangle formed by High Street, George Street and North Street, the majority of the shops being in the High Street. In the middle of the High Street is the Vicarage Field shopping precinct, an unassuming but much appreciated development completed in 1967 containing some thirty shops and the health centre. Behind it is a large car park, one of a number which the council has provided of late, some of them on the sites of demolished buildings. Parking is also allowed on either side of the one-way High Street, a situation which on occasion threatens to get out of hand when delivery vans find themselves with nowhere to deliver or 8-feet-wide buses are expected to squeeze through $7\frac{1}{2}$-feet-wide gaps. When this happens order is rapidly restored by the forces of the law, which in Hailsham consist chiefly of the town's one traffic warden.

The police force proper inhabits a recent and not very striking addition to the town's public buildings, opposite the much better council offices, on a site known as the Deer Paddock. As late as the turn of the century there was indeed a field containing deer on the site, the animals

A view of Hailsham from the church tower, looking north-west along the High Street

sharing it with an ornamental clock-tower erected by Mr Strickland—a familiar name in the town—in honour of Queen Victoria's first jubilee. She had so many it is a wonder civic authorities managed to keep thinking up fresh ways of celebrating them, let alone find the money to finance the junketings, but Hailsham was able to mark a later one with a pair of gates at the High Street entrance to the churchyard. Hailsham's first parish council, which contained three clergymen, was elected in 1898. The first policeman to take up permanent full-time duties arrived some fifty years earlier, following a request from the parish chairman for his transfer from Horsebridge. He was just in time to ensure that the celebrations marking the coming of the railway to the town, in 1849, did not get out of hand, despite which the great day was marred by the death of a passenger who was killed whilst standing on the step of a moving carriage.

The line closed 120 years later, not without considerable objections being raised within the town and in other places through which it passed. An enquiry was held at which it was stated that the population would have to reach a certain figure before the continuation of services could be considered viable. Within a couple of years that figure was reached but by then the tracks had been ripped up and all possibility of the resumption of services gone. It was a rather curious decision when one considers that all those making it had to do was to take a look at the hundreds of homes then under construction in the town and at Polegate, and at the plans approved for many more, but such is often the way with branch line closures. Right up to the end the trains were well patronized and provided the quickest and most convenient means of getting to Eastbourne, or to Polegate for the main London line. The Southdown and Maidstone and District buses are a better substitute than nothing at all but even here, despite the fairly recent erection of a garage in the town, services have been curtailed of late.

Hailsham prospers and continues to expand but an increasing proportion of its centre is given over to the motor car. An ambitious plan exists for the rebuilding of the town with the three main streets becoming pedestrian precincts, a ring road, and a large intersection on the site of the railway station. The pedestrian precinct is an excellent thing but if it is divorced from bus and train services it can only encourage an even greater use of the car, and a very good case could be made for permitting buses to run into the heart of the town, even if one excludes all other vehicles.

There is not a great deal of entertainment to be had in Hailsham in the evening, many of the young people preferring to make for Eastbourne. A cinema existed in George Street but despite some brave attempts at a revival by local enthusiasts it eventually succumbed to bingo, and from time to time entertainments of one sort or another are put on in the secondary school. This latter is an excellent example of an old building which has been extended on a number of occasions, each time in a contemporary style, and yet manages to retain an overall sense of unity. The Women's Institute, the Young Farmers' Club, and other such bodies all have their devotees, whilst probably the greatest influence on the life of Hailsham is still that of the Church.

In effect this means churches. Apart from the Protestant parish church of St Mary's, there is the Roman Catholic St Wilfrid's in South Road, an Independent Free Chapel facing the old railway bridge, a Methodist Chapel in High Street, a Baptist Chapel in Market Street, and a Gospel Mission in Gordon Road.

Father Whatmore, the present Catholic priest, has compiled a painstaking and most detailed history of his parish, which, of course, until the Reformation was centred on St Mary's. In the early thirteenth century the church at Hailsham belonged to Michelham Priory, an Augustinian establishment set up to the west of the town by Gilbert de Laigle, Lord of Pevensey.

Michelham owned a good deal of the Pevensey Marshes and land further afield, but the Black Death killed off eight of its thirteen canons, a blow from which it never really recovered. Before this it had given up its claim on Hailsham to Bayham, but only after a long quarrel. It was dissolved in 1536, probably with more relief than regret,

the prior retiring on a comfortable pension, whilst the canons were all found benefices as parish priests in various parts of Sussex, apart from one who went to St Peter's, Cornhill, London.

Today the priory is in the keeping of the Sussex Archaeological Society. The principal building is the Tudor wing, a delightful house constructed of local sandstone, which is thought to have been recovered from the ruins of the monastic buildings. There is a superb wooden barn, dating from the fourteenth to the sixteenth century, which is now a museum, with some fascinating relics of farming in Sussex before the days of mechanization. The approach to the priory is through the sixty-foot-high stone gatehouse tower, which dates from the last years of the fourteenth century and as such is the oldest remaining part of the priory. It is largely in its original condition and one may still climb to the roof and look across the battlements to the extensive grounds and the Cuckmere winding through them. I once visited Michelham when an archery contest was in progress. It was a scene which completed what is at any time a graceful picture of a beautiful but unpretentious house in a perfect setting.

To return to the history of the church in Hailsham; by 1600 only one man and one woman are recorded as refusing to accept the Protestant faith. As late as the end of the nineteenth century an effigy of the Catholic Priest of St Leonards, to which parish Hailsham then belonged, was

Michelham Priory

burned at the Lewes bonfire celebrations, and it was not until 1915 that the Catholic Mass was again celebrated within the parish of Hailsham, after a break of 356 years. It took place at a house in Upper Dicker, close to Michelham. Because of the persecution of Protestants by 'Bloody Mary' there was still, even at this late date, some feeling against the Roman Catholic faith in Hailsham, and an attempt was made to prevent the erection of a small wooden church in South Road on land which belonged to a Catholic. The vicar put an end to this and nowadays the ecumenical movement is gaining strength in Hailsham as elsewhere.

A population in excess of 10,000 needs rather more than a market and agriculture to keep it occupied and Hailsham is the centre for a number of industries. Some are pursued, with little noise and no apparent pollution, in the new factory estate at the back of Station Road, but the chief one has existed in the town for the best part of 200 years.

Burfield's began making ropes on a site in South Road at the very beginning of the nineteenth century and over the years they supplied clients ranging from the Cunard Steamship Company to the hangman at Lewes Gaol. In 1830 one of their foremen, a Mr Green, set up his own factory a few hundred yards to the north on the far side of what is now the recreation ground, and some twenty years ago the two companies came together. If you have a woven plastic fibre mat on your kitchen floor it may well

Inside a Sussex barn at Michelham

have come from Hailsham, as do a large proportion of the ropes and rigging of boats and ships all over the world.

Until recently sisal was the basic raw material from which the ropes were woven, but changing economic conditions and a world shortage of sisal have brought about an almost complete transfer to synthetic fibres. These start out as crystals which are processed in the Hailsham factory and once converted to fibres can be treated in much the same way as the old natural ones.

Rope-making is very much a mixture of the old and the new. The oldest of the platting machines which whirl and clank around, slowly weaving a rope which can cost anything up to £3,000 and can hold a 100,000 ton supertanker, began its career weaving ropes for the tea clippers in the 1860s.

Something like 10 per cent of the working population of the town is employed in the two factories; a number of them are married women with families for whom the firm makes special arrangements so that they can be at home during school holidays.

The way eastwards out of Hailsham is not by the seemingly direct route along Marshfoot Lane, for in half a mile it becomes all marsh and no lane, but by Battle Road. This heads north until it joins the Lewes to Battle road at Union Corner, whence it continues eastward. Union Corner commemorates the site of the workhouse. Thomas Geering in his *Our Sussex Parish*, published in 1884, paints an almost inviting picture of the Hailsham workhouse, one strikingly different to the universally accepted Dickensian one of unrelieved misery. He writes of the "thriftless unmarried man who all his days had nought to do but live, retiring unabashed to be kept by his more thrifty neighbours"; the "maimed soldier and the worn-out sailor", meeting again "to quid and to smoke and tell oft-told tales of love and war, of lust and rapine"; and of the "unpremeditated humour" of the idiot, setting "the company of idlers, young and old, in a roar of laughter".

The Hailsham workhouse moved from the Market Square to its final site about the time Geering was writing, the previous one having been in use since 1762. Prior to that the poor, infirm and unwanted were lodged in various houses in the town; there must have been a good few of the latter for the parish register for 1740 records that nine out of the thirty-two baptisms carried out that year were of illegitimate births. The district still provides a refuge for the unfortunate, albeit an infinitely more humane one than the old workhouse, in the guise of Hellingly Hospital. This, which deals with mental disorders, is a collection of buildings one mile to the north of Union Corner, and far from being the forbidding, enclosed asylum of Victorian days, is set amidst large and beautifully kept gardens and has no gates or walls separating it from the outside world.

The Pevensey Levels, and the Herstmonceux telescope

Floods on the Pevensey Marshes

Pevensey Marshes refute most emphatically the notion that since the coming of the day-tripper and the motor car isolation has ceased to have meaning in Sussex. It is possible to wander for half a day along the Marsh roads, at times coming to within a mile of the crowded beaches of Pevensey Bay and often within sight of Bexhill, and encounter no more than a dozen vehicles and pass less than half that number of dwellings. The principal inhabitants of the Marshes are sheep, cattle and birds and one cannot imagine that this will ever change. One may sit on a gate or a stile, on a clear, mild winter morning, with the sun low in the sky above Pevensey Castle and moving towards the South Downs which end where the Marshes begin, and hear nothing but the occasional distant rumble of a train or a motorcycle and sometimes the beat of wings as a pair of swans fly overhead on their way from one marsh stream to another. Once the Marshes were covered by the sea and they are still subject to severe flooding, so that at such times it is not difficult to picture how they looked when the Romans built Pevensey Castle or when the Normans began their reclamation in the years immediately after the conquest. The twentieth century has put its mark on the Marshes in the shape of the great dome of the telescope of the Royal Greenwich Observatory at Herstmonceux, but this enhances, rather than detracts from their air of other-worldly timelessness.

The fishing fleet at Hastings with the castle in the background

CHAPTER EIGHT

Hastings to Newhaven

Hastings and Brighton are the hilliest of the Sussex seaside towns and both provide some splendid views. In Hastings the most spectacular is to be had from Castle Hill. To the east one looks over Old Town to the cliffs and open country; inland to the north-west is the centre of the modern town, the vista of rooftops and chimney pots broken by the green square of the Central cricket ground and the high railway embankment beyond; whilst to the south is the sea. Immediately in front are the ruins of the castle and beyond them the ground falls abruptly away revealing the sea stretching to the horizon.

William the Conqueror would have stood on that spot and looked back to Normandy when he returned to Hastings after defeating Harold. We know he spent five days in the town before setting off for London by way of Dover, and it must have been then that he decided to erect a fortress to protect the shipping lanes linking his two kingdoms. It was begun within three years of the Norman Conquest and additions were made at various dates until at least the end of the twelfth century. Yet by the end of the fourteenth it was already falling into decay, a process which has continued until it is now merely a picturesque ruin.

Its decline is linked with that of the town over which it stood. Hastings was an important harbour long before William made it famous and the Romans may possibly have erected fortifications along the cliffs. The name of the town derives from a Saxon tribe, the Haestingas, who settled on the site after the Romans had gone. The harbour they built was situated under the White Rock—which is actually a dirty yellow in colour—close to where the pier now stands, but as the cliffs eroded away the harbour silted up and a new one came into use to the east between the east and west cliffs. It was here that William probably landed after re-embarking at Pevensey.

For a time Hastings was the chief port of England, joining the confederation of the Cinque Ports and being eventually recognized as the most senior of them. King John had a good deal to do with the decline of Hastings, for when he lost Normandy in 1204 much of the town's trade with the Continent went with it. Hastings, along with the other Cinque Ports, once supplied all the ships for the king's navy but by the time of the Armada it could raise only one, the 70-ton *Ann Bonaventure*. In later years the harbour was used only by the fishing fleet. There was an attempt to revive it at the end of the nineteenth century, firstly by the Corporation—until the ratepayers refused to co-operate—and then by private enterprise. A considerable section of quay was erected but both money and enthusiasm ran out long before the scheme was completed, leaving the unfinished western portion jutting out into the sea. A good deal of it remains, although pieces have been washed away, and what is left is of use only as a perch for seagulls and fishermen. Not quite everything was lost, although dignity was certainly a casualty, the site of the one-time premier port of England now being occupied by a children's boating pool.

In one respect Hastings retains its importance. Despite losing its harbour it has kept its fishing fleet and this now has a home on the shingle underneath the East Cliff. Beyond the boats stands the best known feature of Hastings, the net stores. These tall, wooden, sentry-box-like structures with their tarred, slatted slides have featured in innumerable paintings by artists famous and unknown, and in this century have become, through the medium of the poster, almost a symbol of the town. They go back to pre-Elizabethan times and at present there are forty-three of them. Twenty years ago many were in need of repair and it seemed that they might well all disappear, but an increasing awareness of their unique character has provided funds for their renovation and, where necessary, replacement.

They are grouped around what was originally the church of St Nicholas, built in 1854 to serve the fishermen and their families. There were at that time 150 fishing-boats at Hastings. The church was closed on the outbreak of the Second World War, used by the military, and then left empty in 1945. In the spring of 1956 it was most fittingly brought back into use as the Fishermen's Museum. Its principal exhibit is the *Enterprise*, a lugger built at Hastings in 1909.

It may well be that neither the museum nor the preservation of the *Enterprise* would have come about had not a similar boat, the *Industry* of 1870, been deliberately burnt on the beach at Hastings in 1953, being considered of no further use. Burning was the traditional method of disposing of obsolete boats but the *Industry* was an historic vessel. Her destruction stirred preservationists and it was realized that the *Enterprise*, the only surviving Hastings lugger, might well go the same way if action was not taken to save her. Now she stands, fully-rigged, the last of a famous line, and every last Sunday in September a harvest festival service is held from her in memory of the fishermen of Hastings who have lost their lives at sea.

There are some twenty trawlers at Hastings today, built at Newhaven, Rye and Whitstable, plus many smaller boats belonging to part-time and weekend fishermen.

The return of the weekend fishermen makes an entertaining spectacle on a Sunday evening as they make landfall. The boats come spluttering into sight, either around the edge of the old harbour wall or else from the west out of the setting sun, depending upon where the best fishing is to be had, one following another in such close succession that sometimes they have to cruise up and down until sufficient hands are available to haul them in. They are then attached, two at a time, to a cable and pulled up the steeply shelving shingle. In former days this would have been attached to a horse-powered capstan but now a motor driven winch is used. The beach dips so steeply—the rise and fall of the tide at Hastings, twenty-five feet at spring tides, is the greatest on the south coast—that the man operating the winch cannot see the boats at the water's edge and has to trust to the signals of an assistant posted on the brow of the slope. At his command the motor puffs away, the boats come slowly up the beach and into view, each one being stowed in its berth ready for the next weekend.

Until fairly recent times quite large ships anchored off the beach at Hastings and sailing colliers from the northeast unloading their cargoes into small boats was a common sight, still remembered by older inhabitants of the town.

The Old Town, to the east of Hastings' not very distinguished pier, is a mixture of souvenir shops, funfair and snack bars and handsome architecture. The latter is mostly to be found in High Street, which extends from the front for half a mile inland. It begins with a sign marking the site of Seagate in 1385, continues with a launderette, an antique shop, a family planning centre, a beautifully restored Regency terrace, a junk shop specializing in bakelite ashtrays and very old electrical appliances, a butcher's shop, a church, more antique shops and cottages. High Street has not yet become smart in the manner of the lanes in Brighton, with the consequence that one may well find

The fishing fleet returning to Hastings

St Leonards

bits and pieces tossed into the windows of junk shops which elsewhere would be labelled antiques and priced accordingly. Dante Gabriel Rossetti lived for a time in this part of Hastings, and married Elizabeth Siddal (who posed for so many Pre-Raphaelite pictures) in the town. Peter de Wint and David Cox also painted here; Turner's and Constable's connections with the town have already

been touched upon; Samuel Palmer painted Pevensey Bay a few miles to the west; Van Dyck painted Rye; and of the many twentieth-century artists associated with the district, particularly worthy of note are Edward Burra, who lived for many years near Rye, and Sir Thomas Monnington, whose *Stations of the Cross* is in the beautiful parish church at Brede, a few miles to the north-east of the town on the A28 Tenterden road.

St Leonards is the exception to the rule that all Sussex resorts grew out of an existing community, however small. Until James Burton (a London builder and speculator) founded it in the 1820s it was nothing but green fields running down to the sea on the outskirts of Hastings. Long before the great forest which once covered Sussex had extended over the site and beyond, out into what is now the bed of the English Channel, and it was from this that Burton derived the name of his creation. His son, the well-known architect Decimus, designed much of it, its chief feature being the finely laid out Warrior Square.

High buildings flank it on three sides, the fourth being open to the sea; it has been somewhat altered over the years and hardly improved. The promenade at Hastings continues through to St Leonards, there being nothing to indicate where one ends and the other begins—much in the manner of Brighton and Hove—the long façade of boarding-houses and apartment buildings extending in an unbroken line.

One rather sad field, sandwiched between a row of semi-detacheds and a garage, and itself now scheduled to be built upon, is all that separates St Leonards from Bexhill.

This latter was the last of the Sussex resorts to be developed, its population 100 years ago numbering little more than 2,000. Now it is around 33,000, and until the local government changes of 1974 was, in area, the largest borough in Sussex, stretching along the coast from Bulverhythe to Pevensey Sluice, a distance of six miles.

Bexhill possesses an elusive personality. Its brochure, featuring a large picture of the mayor with an accompanying address of welcome, gives a clue to Bexhill attitudes, although it should be added that a description of the town in five languages points to an awareness of a changing world. The French are for some reason the only ones favoured with the information that Bexhill's climate is the envy of all the world. This claim is not as brazen as it sounds for the town is an exceptionally healthy place. It has a lot of sunshine all the year round, very clean air and plenty of sea breezes. Facing due south and far from any high cliffs, it is free of both fierce north winds and clinging sea mists. Thus it is a great place for convalescent homes and invalids; indeed catering for their needs may be said to be Bexhill's chief industry.

It has few others, although it is just possible that it might have become Sussex's answer to Wigan or the Rhondda Valley. In the early nineteenth century certain optimistic speculators, encouraged by the discovery of fibrous lignite on the Hastings side of the village of Bexhill, sunk a mine and a lot of money prospecting for coal. In all they spent around £80,000 but found nothing.

Several decades were to pass before Bexhill expanded beyond the small group of houses clustered around the Norman parish church and the fourteenth-century manor house. These stand a mile back from the sea on a site which dates back to 772. At that time Offa, King of the Angles, signed a deed conferring on Oswald, Bishop of Chichester, the Manor of Bixlea. By the twelfth century it was back in the hands of the bishop and remained there until the Dissolution of the Monasteries. Queen Elizabeth I granted it to Lord Buckhurst and his descendants, the earls of Dorset and De la Warr, are the present owners.

The earls De la Warr are as important in the story of Bexhill as are the Devonshires in that of Eastbourne, for it was the seventh and eighth earls who were responsible for the development of the town. This began in the late 1870s and has continued at a steady pace since then. Because it got going so late Bexhill belongs far less to the Victorian era than do the other Sussex resorts. There is something of the 1920s or '30s about it, chiefly perhaps on account of the De la Warr Pavilion, that famous piece of concrete and glass completed in 1936 and for a long time one of the best known examples of modern architecture in the country.

ERECTED MCMXI KING GEORGE V CORONATION YEAR

The 1911 terrace surmounted by the 1936 De La Warr Pavilion, Bexhill-on-Sea

140

Somehow it has never looked quite right since the Standard Flying Tens, the Hillman Minxes, the young men in wide-bottomed grey flannels and the women in pencil skirts and berets have disappeared from around it.

The entire history of the development of Bexhill as a resort is encompassed in the varying styles of architecture clustered around the De la Warr Pavilion. These range from ornate late Victorian and the hilarious imitation Brighton Pavilion domes of the Bexhill Club, through Edwardian pomposity and inter-war lumpishness to modern decorated functional. Immediately in front of the De la Warr is a bit of frippery erected to mark the coronation of George V in 1912, which in a curious way contains echoes of Lutyens' New Delhi. It is all held together by the sweeping curves of the promenade, seen at their best from the water's edge at low tide, when it is possible to stand far enough back to take it all in.

Westwards from Bexhill a thin line of chalets and caravan-sites divides the Pevensey Levels from the shingle and the sea. Once a great haunt of smugglers, Pevensey itself is still an old-fashioned, unspoilt village, dominated by its magnificent castle and quite separate from the twentieth-century ephemera of Normans Bay and Pevensey Bay.

Eastbourne might well claim that it is the most popular of all Sussex resorts, for it possesses a greater number of hotels and boarding-houses than any other. There is said to exist a rivalry between Eastbourne and Brighton, but beyond the fact that both are beside the sea there is little comparison. Eastbourne would shudder if asked to approve some of the goings-on which Brighton cheerfully tolerates; instead it sets out to cater for those who want to spend a holiday, or their retirement, in peaceful, well-ordered, dignified surroundings. It is possible to describe Eastbourne as dull, which one could never do of Brighton, but it is only so in the context of not offering that which it has no wish to.

There can be few, if any, towns which are cleaner than Eastbourne. Almost all the large hotels along the promenade present spotlessly white façades to the sea, as though daring it to attempt to sully them. It does its best, sometimes working itself up into a great fury, throwing shingle and spray against them, but they remain aloof and seemingly untouched. The most splendid of them are to be found west of the pier along the Grand Parade which extends to the foot of Beachy Head. Eastwards they grow smaller, steadily diminishing in size, but all equally well cared-for. The promenade at this end of the town used to feature a miniature tramway but the last few years have seen great changes hereabouts.

Between Pevensey Bay and Eastbourne is the Crumbles, a low promontory, formerly an expanse of wasteland practically deserted all the year round other than by a rich variety of birds and their attendant

The Promenade at Eastbourne, looking towards Langney

birdwatchers. The most prominent building was a Martello tower, one of six between Pevensey Bay and Beachy Head, the survivors of fourteen erected as defence against the expected invasion by Napoleon, and named after a similar fortification at Mortella Point, Corsica, which had withstood a severe bombardment by British forces in 1793. Now the Crumbles has been transformed, there is a large indoor swimming pool, a marina is planned, and much of the former wasteland is taken up by an estate of privately-owned houses. The tramway has been lifted and sent off to Seaton and the promenade has been extended to curve inland around Princes Park, past a coach station and on alongside the new estate to come out on the main A259 Eastbourne to Hastings road at Langney. This latter district has also expanded enormously, growing from a small collection of houses set between open fields and the wastelands of the Crumbles to a sizeable suburb with a large shopping centre.

One might wonder where all these new inhabitants of Eastbourne find employment, for although the town provides a home for many retired people, those living on the new estates are mostly young married couples with small children. Some have jobs in the holiday industry but a great many work in the trading estates at Hampden Park, a mile to the north-west of Langney, or go further afield to Hailsham, Brighton or even London.

The advent of so many young people to Eastbourne has meant a shift in emphasis, reducing the town's preoccupation with the middle-aged and elderly. After a long period of stagnation the population is increasing. It went up from 58,000 in 1951 to 71,000 in 1971, and it is planned that it should continue to grow until all the low-lying land between the present north-eastern extremity and Hampden Park is built over. Hampden Park is an earlier residential development, sprawling behind the town and beneath the Downs and linking Eastbourne with Polegate, whence the three miles to the town centre is a continuously built-up area. It is a pity that the fields within the town boundaries, now totally encompassed by buildings but still grazed by sheep and cattle, have to go, but better this than an unplanned sprawl deep into the countryside. Already a large, extremely well-appointed hospital has been built, although financial cutbacks have meant that it is only half the size originally intended.

Anyone who assumes that Eastbourne is entirely a creation of the Victorian era will be somewhat surprised if he departs from the familiar route between the railway and the coach stations and the promenade and ventures into the hinterland. There, beyond the red brick villas, is Old Town. At the heart of this is the parish church of St Mary, a good part of which has stood since the twelfth century. Next door is the sixteenth-century parsonage, whilst opposite is the former manor house, which dates from the eighteenth century and is now the home of the Towner

Art Gallery. The most handsome art gallery on the South Coast, it was acquired by the Corporation after the First World War. Set on sloping ground and surrounded by extensive gardens, it displays within its spacious rooms a permanent collection of nineteenth- and twentieth-century pictures; in addition there is nearly always a temporary or travelling exhibition of interest.

But Eastbourne goes back further still. Behind St Mary's is Motcombe Gardens; within the gardens is a small lake and flowing out of the lake is a stream or bourne. Here are the town's origins, for 2,500 years ago the predecessors of the present citizens took up residence around the bourne. They were Celts and were the first of many races who have inhabited this part of Sussex. The Romans came and built a large villa, the remains of which were discovered down by the sea in the eighteenth century, and they in turn gave way to the Saxons. Under Saxon rule the area was known as the "Hundred of Burne." The Normans, in the *Domesday Book*, called it "Borne," and by the middle of the sixteenth century the name "East Bourne" was in common use. There was also a South Bourne, a district through which the stream flowed on its way to the sea. The bourne is now an underground sewer but its path can be traced along South Street, emerging on to the beach east of the pier beside Marine Parade. This latter was known until the mid-nineteenth century as "Sea Houses", after the fishermen's cottages which stood on the shore, although very much grander dwellings already existed at that time, four of George III's children spending their time at Sea Houses in 1780.

Royal patronage ensured the town's future as a resort, but development did not begin on a significant scale for another seventy years. The railway arrived in 1849 and two years earlier the Duke of Devonshire commissioned James Berry to draw up a plan for the town; this combination transformed Eastbourne.

The various family names of the Devonshires loom large in the story of Eastbourne over the last 250 years, and are today commemorated in many parts of the town. Their first appearance was in 1723 when Sir Spencer Compton, Speaker of the House of Commons, acquired the land on which most of the western and central areas of Eastbourne now stand. His daughter, to whom the estate passed, married Lord Cavendish, the son of the third Duke of Devonshire, and it was the seventh Duke, William Cavendish, who died in 1891, who was chiefly responsible for the nineteenth-century growth of Eastbourne.

He advanced loans of up to 75 per cent to builders prepared to follow Berry's plans, and found no shortage of takers. At least two went bankrupt, but the town continued to grow regardless, the population during the latter part of the nineteenth century increasing from 3,453 to over 53,000. In the sixty years subsequent to 1900 it rose by no more than a further 10,000, an indication of how truly

Victorian in character Eastbourne is, or at least was until the present decade.

Eastbourne's air of leisured gentility, of carefully planned and skilfully executed exclusiveness, remains, although some jarring notes have been struck of late, where some of the large villas set in extensive grounds have been demolished and their places taken by still expensive but timidly dull blocks of luxury flats. The tallest of these and the one which has always caused the most controversy stands on the front immediately below the Downs. Its height, taken along with its commanding position, ensures that it not only dominates the west end of the town but also the view of the entire skyline of Eastbourne, whether seen from above up on the Downs or inland from the Pevensey Marshes. There is a strong case to be made for using up surplus land around large houses, or even knocking them down to provide a larger number of smaller homes, and at the same time preventing the encroachment upon the countryside. Such considerations hardly applied in this case, however, and it would be a shame if it created a precedent and brought about the destruction of the special character of the district.

The Duke, or rather his image, still watches over his creation in the form of a statue by Sir W. Goscombe John, erected at the junction of Devonshire Place and the Grand Parade in the last year of Queen Victoria's reign.

Whilst the building of the town proceeded apace, the sea continued to remind the citizens that even a duke was mortal and no match for the forces of nature should they take it into their heads to grow boisterous. Considerable damage was done during a storm in 1878 and work was immediately begun on extending the sea wall. By 1882 the builder called a halt and a wrangle ensued with the local Board, the former claiming that the latter had made his task extremely difficult by its failure to provide sufficient protection in the way of breakwaters, groynes and so on. Meanwhile the sea obligingly added point to the builder's case by washing away 900 feet of his newly-erected wall. The courts found in his favour but the House of Lords gave final judgement in favour of the Board. At this point the Board of Guardians became a Town Corporation and took over the work of defending their charge against the sea, the sea wall being completed by their surveyor.

A corporation needs a town hall and, after heated exchanges between various parties a site was selected not far from the Duke's residence, Compton Place. Mr W. Tadman Foulkes's plans (somewhat modified) were chosen and in 1884 work on the pink brick and Portland stone building was begun. Like so much of Victorian and Edwardian Eastbourne it is boldly assertive, a trifle vulgar, perhaps, through trying too hard to appear aristocratic, but its well-scrubbed façade is full of interesting ornamental detail. It stands opposite what I had always assumed was another impressive piece of late Victoriana,

Cricket at the Saffrons County Ground, Eastbourne, with the Town Hall in the background

146

the Roman Catholic Church of Our Lady of Ransom, until I discovered that it actually dates from the inter-war years; nevertheless it has very much the atmosphere of the Victorian era, being dark and mysterious within.

As important to a seaside town as its town hall and its churches is its pier. No one doubted that Eastbourne should have one, but with the inevitability that seemed to accompany any great scheme in the town there was much squabbling over its site. Eventually in 1866 it was begun opposite the junction of the Marine and Grand Parades. The ravages of the sea and the march of progress ensured that it was still being added to in the twentieth century.

A feature of the streets of Eastbourne some 100 years ago, and one hardly calculated to encourage visitors, was snakes. The countryside around, with its abundance of long grass, thick hedgerows, shady trees and mild climate, provides a natural habitat for the adder and the grass-snake. Building was then going on at such a rate that pockets of land remained undeveloped for some time whilst the boundaries of the town were pushed further outwards and it was quite common to find a snake marooned on a newly laid pavement. The holidaymaker of today need hardly expect such encounters; if he looks very hard he may find a grass-snake on the Downs behind Beachy Head, and I once nearly ran over one sunning itself in the middle of a lane near Polegate, but they are shy creatures and like to keep away from people. The

Eastbourne Pier

147

poisonous adder also exists in the district but is even warier than the grass-snake and is hardly ever seen.

Eastbourne parks can be guaranteed free of such reptiles. Instead, their inhabitants are of the more generally accepted varieties. The friendliest squirrel I ever saw appeared in the middle of the bowling-green at Motcombe Gardens one morning last summer. It looked around, took in the bowlers, ran over to a bowl, stood up on its hind legs and tried to push it with its front ones. Eventually giving up the struggle to make off with this giant-size nut, it sauntered over to a couple sitting beside the green and for some time accepted pieces of sandwich from the wife whilst the husband crouched beside it clicking away with his camera. The squirrel only returned to the trees when it was obvious there was nothing else on offer.

Like the town itself the parks and gardens are all beautifully kept. Throughout the season the carpet gardens, set between the roadway and the promenade of the Grand Parade, are a blaze of constantly changing colour. Motcombe Gardens are the oldest municipal ones, whilst the largest are those at Hampden Park. These latter were once marshland and a haunt of wildfowl. They were taken over by the borough in 1911 and in the following year laid out and opened to the public; wild geese can still be seen on the lake.

Devonshire Park is the most central and the least attractive because of the variety of uses to which its restricted space is put. The tennis-courts are said to be second only to Wimbledon and Davis Cup matches are held on them. Also within the park's boundaries are three theatres. The Devonshire Park Theatre is the home of the repertory company, whilst the 2,000-seat Congress Theatre next door stages anything from an amateur dramatic show to a performance by the Count Basie Band, the Royal Ballet or the Conservative Party Conference. The Congress is the largest of the modern public buildings in the centre of the town and was completed in 1963. Its exterior is neither controversial nor exciting but internally it is excellent with fine acoustics. Behind the Congress is the Old Winter Gardens. This was put up in the mid-1870s and has an attractive atmosphere, typical of its period, created by light filtering down from a glass dome; it would be even nicer if some potted palms could be introduced. The Winter Gardens caters for a variety of interests, including wrestling and old-time dancing, although not on the same nights. The fourth of the town's theatres, the Royal Hippodrome, stands just behind the pier; it specializes in old-time music-hall. Between them Eastbourne's theatres give a very good clue to the tastes of the inhabitants and the visitors.

Until recently there was a fifth theatre. This stood at the end of the pier but was damaged by fire and although repaired is no longer used as such. It originally opened in 1901 and in its Edwardian heyday such celebrities as Mrs

Patrick Campbell and Lily Langtry played upon its boards. The theatre has gone but fortunately the damage has been repaired and the pier stands restored, all in white, the very epitome of seaside Victoriana, perfect in its way and the loveliest of all the Sussex piers.

The most popular of Eastbourne's live entertainment centres is the bandstand. Set in the middle of the Grand Parade and built out over the beach, it can seat 3,500 people in three tiers facing out to sea. The finest bands in the country, military and civil, play there throughout the long season which lasts from early spring to late autumn.

Now, after half a century during which little in the town altered following its leap forward in the previous 50 years, Eastbourne is again undergoing change. It cannot expand to the west where Beachy Head bars its way, but it can and is expanding to the north and the east. It is still much favoured as a place of retirement but the majority of people moving to Eastbourne are much younger, many attracted from London by property values sufficiently lower to make the move worthwhile. Yet one cannot see a radical alteration in the character of the town and it may be supposed that Eastbourne will continue along its chosen path, combining a sense of decorum with a finely calculated awareness of just what it takes to bring the visitors returning in their tens of thousands each year.

That Cuckmere Haven is something special is instantly obvious. On a coastline which has been intensely devel-

Birling Gap and the Seven Sisters. Note the winch for hauling up boats from the beach below

oped it is remarkable to find so untouched and so seemingly natural a scene as the winding course of the River Cuckmere through the beautiful valley from Alfriston, across the main coast road by the vanished village of Exceat and out to the sea between the high cliffs of the Seven Sisters and Seaford Head. In fact the idyllic state of

149

the Cuckmere Valley and the coastline thereabouts probably represents a more intensive effort by men than anything else on the Sussex coast.

Before the Second World War there had been attempts to develop the site, attempts which were thwarted partly by luck, partly by the National Trust and similarly dedicated people. Since 1935 the East Sussex County Council

The Southdowns Way at Cuckmere Haven

began to take an interest in its preservation and this culminated in the acquisition of 692 acres to form the Seven Sisters Country Park in 1971. The coastline between Eastbourne and Seaford, embracing Beachy Head, the Seven Sisters, Cuckmere Haven and Seaford Head is known as the Sussex Heritage Coast, which means, in the words of the East Sussex County Planning Officer, that the "Countryside Commission recognizes both its natural renown and the need to maintain its character". Thirdly there is the eighty-mile-long South Downs Way which begins at Eastbourne and takes alternative routes to Alfriston, one via Willingdon and Jevington, the other—a spectacular but gruelling trek along the very undulating top of the Seven Sisters and then through the Cuckmere Valley. From Alfriston the Way continues along the brow of the Downs to the Hartings and the Hampshire border.

All of this attention has meant that the area is preserved forever from development. To enjoy it one has to leave one's car and walk, or possibly cycle or ride a horse, and it is extraordinary how many walkers one encounters in even a brief period. But it is not the intention that the area should be preserved in a state of suspended animation. Nature makes this impossible even if it were desirable; furthermore, although the park and the Heritage Coast were created with visitors in mind, thousands of people live within them and their needs and convenience have to be considered and catered for.

Such care for the Sussex coastline and countryside would have greatly pleased two men who did much to encourage an enlightened attitude to such matters. Arthur Beckett was the founder and longest-serving editor of the *Sussex County Magazine*; the Rev. A. A. Evans, Vicar of East Dean and Friston from 1908 to 1929, was one of its most prolific contributors. Neither had any illusions that the Sussex seen by the visitor was the same as that of the native, or that a picturesque rural scene might not be the creation of underpaid, overworked men and their families, living in slum conditions, their livelihood subject, in some cases, to the whim of a feckless employer. Beckett and Evans approved of the benefits twentieth-century technology could bring, but they campaigned fiercely against indiscriminate development and speculation. Liberal-minded and humanitarian, they were not very fond of fox-hunting, motorists who drove about indiscriminately on the Downs, or aerodromes. Occasionally they went overboard, criticizing rather too harshly all motorists, whilst some of the speculative building they condemned has been so well absorbed into its setting that one wonders what all the fuss was about. One group of houses (not, as far as I know, condemned by Evans) was a development near East Hoathly in the early 1930s which brought central heating (a rare luxury), electricity (by no means universal) and other conveniences to isolated country people. Forty years later these cottages,

A group of twentieth-century cottages at East Hoathly

deep in the lush Wealden countryside and almost engulfed by luxuriant vegetation in summer, have the look of something as permanent and long-established as the Downs.

One of Beckett's boldest gestures was to print Radclyffe Hall's portrait as the frontispiece of the June 1934 edition of the *Sussex County Magazine*, and refer to her "fighting so strenuously for the life and freedom of her book *The*

Well of Loneliness", brave words for a book sympathetic to lesbianism. Radclyffe Hall's concern "for the welfare of infants, the aged poor, and for the care and protection of the animals she loves" was also noted. The *Sussex County Magazine* was something out of the ordinary and is still much missed.

Seaford is the smallest of the Sussex resorts with a mere twenty hotels and boarding-houses large enough to warrant mention in the 1971 census, and of these the largest and the most handsome was virtually destroyed by fire in the summer of 1976. Its seafront is remarkably undeveloped, with three short, isolated terraces of hotels and flats in the middle and a lot of what is virtually waste ground on either side. Of late there has been some building to the west behind the promenade and some more to the east, up towards the cliffs, but it is mostly residential. The front lacks many of the features found elsewhere at Sussex resorts; there is no pier, no café, no amusement arcade, no beach shops, no deckchairs. Although it has a railway station, at the end of a branch line from Lewes, the only through trains to London are during the morning and evening peaks and there is no direct motor-coach link with the capital outside the summer season.

There has to be a reason for such backwardness—or sensible lack of exploitation, depending upon one's point of view—and it is largely a combination of the forces of nature and the proximity of Eastbourne and Brighton. In medieval times Seaford was much more important, being a corporate member of the Cinque Ports. Its names derives from the ford across the River Ouse, the mouth of which it used to stand beside until the latter was diverted to Newhaven during a great storm around 1540. The disappearance of the river finished Seaford as a place of any importance. Its parliamentary representation remained for a good many more years—William Pitt the Elder was one of its members—but it lost this too in 1832. There was no royal patronage for Seaford and towards the end of the nineteenth century, when the other Sussex resorts were growing rapidly, it ceased to be a borough.

One factor holding back Seaford's development is actually its most spectacular attraction. The lie of the land, the tides and the prevailing winds on occasion combine to produce ferocious storms. At such time the promenade takes a fearful hammering; pebbles from the beach are hurled across the road and waves crashing against it send spray flying above the roofs of the four- and five-storey buildings. Consequently it is almost impossible to keep the façades of these latter in good repair, and hence the almost total absence of promenade hotels. In such conditions a car parked along the promenade suffers permanent damage in a matter of minutes, and anyone sufficiently foolhardy to venture out must keep a firm hold on the railings if he is to maintain his balance; he will in any case be soaked through in seconds. The effect created by the rollers as

The Promenade at Seaford

153

they approach the sea wall, hurl themselves against it and dissolve into a mountain of cascading spray is tremendous.

Seaford Bay has seen many shipwrecks. One of the worst occurred late in the afternoon of Thursday 7th December 1809. Britain being at war with France, most ships travelled in convoy, and a fleet of twenty-five merchantmen was proceeding up Channel under the protection of the sloop *Harlequin*. The ships had already been buffeted by a hurricane and although the wind abated slightly, sleet and fog made conditions still worse. The *Harlequin* had only a vague idea of its position, its captain, Lieutenant Anstruther, believing himself to be off Beachy Head. In the fog he turned towards land and before he could correct his error the *Harlequin* ran aground. Six of the convoy, following closely, did likewise. The crew of the sloop managed to fire a warning gun which saved the others, but those boats aground were pounded to pieces. Anyone who has experienced a Seaford Bay storm may readily appreciate the fearful conditions which prevailed on that December evening.

A crowd assembled on the beach, but although within earshot of the ships and the men clinging to them no one could attempt a rescue until daylight. Then many were saved; either by lines floated ashore or dropped from the cliffs; by people clinging to wreckage; or in the case of a woman and two children aboard the *Harlequin* who had been forgotten when the ship had been abandoned, by a number of rescued sailors who rowed back through the mountainous seas in a small boat to get them off.

By no means everyone lived and not everyone on the shore was there out of compassion. The wreckers, who appeared whenever there was likelihood of booty being washed up, brushed aside pleas for help and seized whatever they could lay their hands on. The wilier ones made off with the goods, but others smashed open casks of spirits and wines and drank themselves insensible on the beach. In all, thirty-four men were drowned, most of them Prussians from the *February* and the *Mithredracht*.

In modern times there have been frequent instances of the Newhaven-Dieppe ferry running into trouble, although since its inception in 1825 there has been only one instance of passengers or crew losing their lives. That was in 1887 when the paddle steamer *Victoria* ran into rocks off Dieppe and nineteen of those aboard were drowned. As recently as the night of 16th January 1974 the car ferry found itself in difficulties. At the time storms were raging all around the British Isles and they were mountainous in Seaford Bay. Heavy lorries and cars on board the ferry were thrown about and one juggernaut was hurled across the deck, crushing cars in its path. Its driver was asleep in the cab and narrowly escaped death. The ship eventually limped into Newhaven hours late, its bruised and weary passengers full of praise for the captain's skilful handling of the dreadful conditions.

P.S. Ryde, *the last of the South-Coast paddle steamers, at Newhaven*

The sea wall at Seaford, despite being of massive construction, is under constant surveillance and is something of a drain on the rates. Sections of the town, although some way back from the sea, lie below high-water mark, so any breach of the wall would be disastrous. The town is centred around the site of the old harbour; there is nothing left of this and not much that is very old elsewhere other than the parish church of St Leonard, parts of which are Norman. Excavations started in 1976 and still going on revealed the foundations of a number of medieval buildings.

Seaford is a great place for boarding-schools. Up on the edge of the cliffs below Seaford Head is the College of Education (formerly the Ladies' College) which occupies a handsome house, the original part being nearly 300 years old, and there are many other schools of varying sizes and offering varying standards of education in the town. A mile or so out of Seaford on the Alfriston road is one of the finest views in all Sussex. On a clear day one may look out from the summit on the Downs across the bay almost to France, whilst at night the reflection upon the water of the flashing beams of Beachy Head lighthouse evoke an atmosphere in which one would require little imagination to convince oneself that amongst the shadows can be seen the dark outline of a smuggler's schooner pursued by an excise cutter.

My first recollection of Newhaven is immediately after the Second World War. No resort was at its best then, after six summers without visitors and six winters without maintenance, aside from any damage brought about by the enemy; and Newhaven, which was never a resort and even now does not really cater for visitors, was in a sorry state. In those days an expedition to the seaside was a major event and my mother, who had been looking forward to the trip to Newhaven for weeks, has scarcely yet forgiven the place for being such a let-down.

But for those interested in boats and harbours. Newhaven can never be dull. It is not a particularly ancient port, having come into existence when the Ouse changed course and by-passed Seaford in the sixteenth century. The village of Meeching changed its name to Newhaven, although the old name survives and is commemorated in a Sealink tug stationed in the harbour. Trade fluctuated and the harbour works were chiefly directed towards preventing shingle silting up the mouth of the river. Finally, in Victorian times, engineering skills and sufficient money to finance the projects made possible the creation of the modern Newhaven. A groyne erected by the harbourmaster, William Stevens, doubled the water level at the entrance, and in 1849 the London, Brighton and South Coast Railway inaugurated the service around which Newhaven's continuing prosperity has been built, the cross-channel link with Dieppe. Ocean-going ships also sailed regularly from Newhaven at this time, one of the best known being the *Alastor*. If one studies shipping

Newhaven

One of the largest ships to call regularly at Newhaven, the container ship Liebenwalde

records one is struck by the large proportion which never survive to reach the breaker's yard; the *Alastor's* longevity is remarkable. She was a barque of 874 gross tons, built at Sunderland in 1875 for R. H. Penney of Shoreham. Between 1877 and 1890 she sailed ten times to New Zealand from Shoreham and Newhaven, taking between 96 and 125 days for the outward leg of the ten voyages. Her career during this, her heyday, was unusually uneventful to the extent that it is said that during one voyage "a good-natured sailor volunteered for a couple of sticks of tobacco to fall overboard in order to vary the monotony". In 1896 she was sold and for over forty years worked under various Scandinavian flags. She came back to England at the outbreak of the Second World War, afterwards serving as a floating restaurant in Ramsgate harbour, and was finally broken up in 1952 at the ripe old age of seventy-seven.

By the end of the nineteenth century the Brighton Railway Company had spent over £½ million at Newhaven, the most spectacular of the works being the 1,000-yard-long western breakwater. To stand at the end of this, especially on a rough day, is very like being in the middle of the Channel; at the height of a storm seas break right over the breakwater lighthouse and anything not embedded in the concrete structure would be swept instantly into oblivion.

The western cliffs behind the breakwater and overlooking the undeveloped area of shingle which serves as Newhaven's beach once formed part of the port's fortifications, with tunnels built into them and blockhouse and gun enplacements dotted about their surface. The remains of these massive and extensive works, which were last used in the Second World War, are falling into decay. In front of them, overlooking the harbour entrance, two rows of houses with space beneath them to keep boats have been built. Their siting, far from other residential property, is an adventurous move and provides the lucky occupiers with a marvellous view of the sea, the sweep of the Seven Sisters beyond Seaford and the constant movement of shipping.

Great ports such as Southampton and Liverpool offer the spectacle of great liners and tankers which a smaller port like Newhaven can never equal, but it has the advantage of being accessible. One may sit outside a dockside pub on the west quay and watch an old tall-funnelled dredger scraping about at the harbour bottom whilst fishing-boats and pleasure-boats putter past, ballast rattles out of a hopper into a lorry, battered and dented from a thousand such encounters, a crane dips towards the deck of a coaster from Scandinavia and removes a stack of timber, and a swan glides towards the bank and is transformed from effortless elegance to undignified scramble as it waddles about ill-temperedly searching for food on the mud-flats beside the swing-bridge. The constant rumble of traffic across the timbers of the old bridge was perhaps the most distinctive of all the waterside sounds of Newhaven; it ceased in 1976 when its much needed successor was opened.

As in all long-established ports, Newhaven has developed piecemeal and the quayside is a ramshackle place, a litter of buildings of all shapes and conditions in a variety of materials; red and yellow brick, corrugated iron, asbestos, concrete and wood, some new, most old, very few without additions, almost as many with bits removed or derelict, glass gone from windows or else so grimy as to be opaque. An old railway-carriage painted grey all over and minus its wheels has been set down to serve as a hut beside the British Rail workshops, and where The London and Paris—the one really grand hotel in Newhaven—used to stand are now piled rows of containers beside the approach to the car ferry.

The largest surviving hotel, The Sheffield, overlooks the ranks of yachts and pleasure-boats tied up in their basin on the west quay, whilst the oldest is The Bridge in the middle of the town. It proclaims in bold lettering for all to see, as they approach down the steep hill from the west, that it was built in 1623 and that Louis Philippe stayed there in 1848 on his arrival in Newhaven after losing the throne of France.

Residential hotels are few in Newhaven and the only people who stay in the town are travellers, yachtsmen, sailors and fishermen, although there are caravan-sites nearby. Newhaven is a great place for fishing, whether it be from the harbour or from a small boat bobbing about all weekend in the Channel, waiting for a bite. Sea-fishing has its hazards, for if a storm springs up Newhaven can be a very difficult port to get back into, and it has been known for a fishing-boat to find survival touch and go. An acquaintance of mine once had to run before the wind along the length of the Sussex coast and right around Dungeness before finding calmer water off Romney Marshes, where he was able to ride out the storm.

Notwithstanding the hazards of the sea, Newhaven's relative proximity to both the sea and the Continent have ensured its prosperity. It was at its busiest during the two world wars; in the first it was the principal supply base for the Western Front, and in the second a centre for hospital ships and RAF rescue launches, which first went into action during the Battle of Britain; I remember seeing them laid up in the years immediately after the war and some still remain, converted to houseboats. Containerization and car ferries have brought further trade and greater congestion on the roads. Although passenger trains provide a regular and speedy service from the quayside to the heart of London, and there is a considerable traffic of new motor vehicles both for import and export through the port by rail, it seems a pity that more effort has not been made to persuade the container operators to use British

FOR PROPERTY TO BE
DEVELOPED
ON THIS SITE AND IN
THE SURROUNDING AREA
CONTACT
J. HARKNESS & SON L^{TD}
DEVELOPERS
PHONE PEACEHAVEN 3177

Peacehaven

Rail instead of sending their huge vehicles along roads ill-equipped to cope with them.

From Newhaven the coast road climbs up to the top of the cliffs and through the gateway into that curious, unlovely place, Peacehaven. So much has been said against it that one instinctively feels one ought to find something to say in its defence. I have never lived there, although I have known people who have, and I have passed through it dozens of times. For all its lack of style and its inelegance, property there is eagerly sought after, as it always has been, chiefly on account of its proximity to Brighton and the sea. In its early days it had the merit—its only merit—of enabling people to buy retirement homes beside the sea at a price they might not have been able to afford elsewhere; nowadays there is no such thing as cheap building-land in Sussex, and prices in Peacehaven are as high as parts of Brighton, Worthing and Eastbourne.

Starting out after the Second World War under the hardly less fanciful title of Anzac-on-Sea, on account of an Australian and New Zealand military camp which had first occupied the site, Peacehaven grew as a jumble of unplanned, unmade streets, running at right angles seawards and inland from the main Brighton to Newhaven road. A number of the plots were bought up by a national newspaper and offered as competition prizes. A good few were never taken up, which explains why gaps remain to this day. The whole place still wears a somewhat impermanent air, a cross between a sort of vast holiday-camp and a caravan-site without the caravans. Slowly, with the erection of shops and pubs and other facilities, the feeling one used to have every time one drove through it that a particularly violent Channel gale might blow the whole thing away is becoming less acute, and much tighter regulations than those which existed in the 1920s and early '30s ensure that all the gaps must be filled before there is any possibility of it spreading further. For all that, I fear the best I can say of Peacehaven is that it is very handy for Brighton.

CHAPTER NINE

Chichester to Hove

Of all the contrasts to be found in Sussex none is greater than that of the two communities on Thorney Island. West Thorney is the most south-westerly parish in the county and was for long one of the most remote. There was once an East Thorney but this has been lost to the sea like so much of this part of Sussex. Just how isolated a life the Thorney Islanders endured, even as late as Victorian times, can be gauged by the fact that there was no road to the outside world until 1870. The Rev. C. Q. Phillipson, rector from 1955 to 1962, has recorded that the causeway which linked Thorney with the Hampshire town of Emsworth was "only completely uncovered at low water during the spring tides. At normal low water it was nearly a foot deep".

In fact Thorney was probably more accessible by water, being only five miles from Portsmouth and ten from the Isle of Wight, both of which are easily seen; the former beyond low-lying Hayling Island and Langstone Har-

bour; the latter across Spithead. The southernmost tip of Thorney is two miles from the open sea, access to it being by way of Emsworth and Chichester Harbours, between which Thorney is set. So the Thorney Islanders may not have been as cut off from the great national events as many seemingly less remote inland areas and over the centuries must have been witness to many of the comings and goings at Portsmouth and Southampton.

Thorney remained a peaceful, sparsely-populated spot until the 1930s. Up until that time the island had merely been in close proximity to the upheavals each war had caused, now the Nazi threat brought the greatest upheaval in its history.

The flat expanses of the West Sussex coastline between the Downs and the sea made ideal landing grounds for air-craft, and in the years immediately before the Second World War the RAF built aerodromes at Ford, Tangmere and Thorney. Virtually the whole of Thorney Island was taken over by the Air Ministry and the station remained in commission for forty years.

The parish church of St Nicholas, dating from around 1200, and the few cottages on the south-easternmost edge of the island were engulfed by the RAF. The road to them crosses the main runway. I tried to visit the church a few years back, as the public was supposedly allowed to, but was politely but firmly told by the LAC at the gate that it was not possible to do so on that particular day. Latterly

A Hercules aircraft taking off from West Thorney

the RAF operated Hercules transport aircraft, their bulbous fuselages slung beneath high wings being a familiar sight in the skies around the Selsey Peninsula.

In 1976 the RAF left Thorney Island and handed it over to the Royal Navy. In the spring of 1977 I tried my luck again and this time the sailor on duty at the main gate wrote me out a pass to visit the church provided I returned

within the hour; whether my wife, our three boys and myself would have been incarcerated in a hulk off Spithead if we had exceeded our time limit I did not attempt to discover. We drove past a great many Services buildings, the construction of which has the familiar faint echo of the Georgian municipal style; passed close to the huge, closed-up hangars and over the runway. Next came a school, a petrol station, more barrack blocks, rows of married quarters, and finally almost at the water's edge on the eastern tip of the island, the church.

St Nicholas's is a small building with flint rubble walls, dressed with Caen-stone. It is beautifully cared for, as one would expect of a Services church. A window in the north wall records the RAFs forty-year significant—if fleeting in terms of the church's history—links. The pulpit was presented by the Air Navigation School in 1962 and on the north side of the churchyard rest the bodies of Commonwealth and German airmen. The waters of Chichester Harbour wash against the bank on which the eastern wall of the churchyard is built. Beside the church the Victorian vicarage stood empty, with a large Navy pantechnicon in the drive, and amongst all the impressive array of Services installations and paraphernalia the only signs of life were two children who came through a gap in the hedge by the vicarage, and a couple of elderly ladies in a Mini on their way, like us, to the church.

The history of architecture in Sussex, like much else,

may be said to begin at Chichester, for the Roman wall is the oldest surviving structure of any substance. Work on it began towards the end of the second century and continued off and on for the best part of 100 years. A good deal survives, the largest section extending for several hundred yards, standing 15 feet high and of sufficient width to allow several people to walk abreast.

From the top of the wall one may look across 1,800 years of history. Beneath one's feet are Roman flints and mortar, whilst to the south is the cathedral, built on the site of the Saxon church of St Peter, its oldest stones dating from the eleventh century, its latest yet to be delivered. Between the walls and the cathedral is a road lined on one side by unpretentious modern two- and three-storey terrace houses and on the other by the extensive offices of the West Sussex County Council. The latter date from the 1930s and are in a rather dull neo-Georgian style—first cousins of Thorney Island barracks—softened and partly obscured by a number of well-placed mature trees. Much more exciting are some recent additions which include a circular-shaped library and the county architect's offices. The latter are of red brick and slate and just right for their location; which is as it should be of course, except that quite often it is not. At the front of the council buildings, facing the cathedral, is the original, handsome Council House, dating from the early eighteenth century.

On the opposite side of the city walls are the back-gardens of the terrace houses of Chichester's Victorian suburbs. The houses were threatened with demolition some years ago; it would be sad if the threat materialized for the long gardens, some rather overgrown and variously filled with rose bushes, creepers, lines of washing, children's swings and all manner of flowers, perfectly set off the crowded town centre. They would surely be considered an uneconomic use of space and would no doubt go too if the houses to which they belong were knocked down.

Chichester Cathedral was begun about 1080, consecrated just over 100 years later, and has, in its essential form, remained unchanged ever since. However, it has suffered damage and been repaired and altered in detail many times, and of late it had become obvious to the most casual visitor that much of the stonework was badly weathered. This was merely the visual evidence of much greater decay, and in 1965 an appeal to raise £700,000 to save the cathedral from eventual dereliction was made. There had been other such crises in its long history, and two fires in the twelfth century caused great damage; in 1861 there was the spectacular collapse of the spire.

For some time it had been realized that the spire was very weak and precautions had been taken so that no one was injured. Nevertheless when the collapse came it was very sudden. So far as is known there was only one eyewitness, a signaller on duty at the semaphore tower in

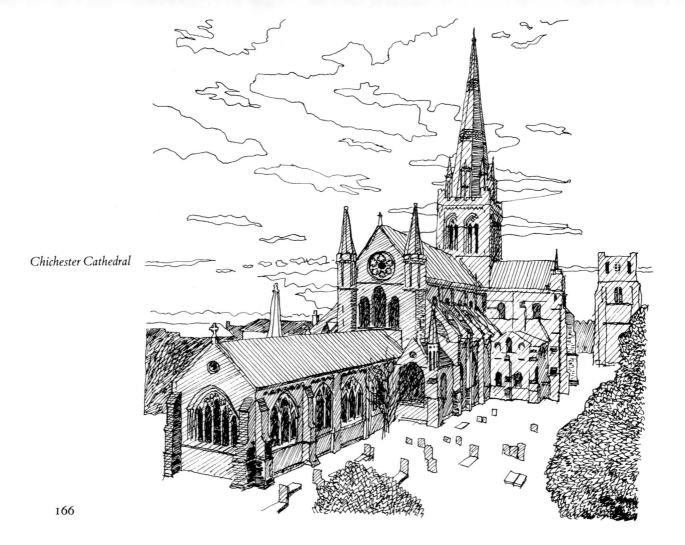

Chichester Cathedral

Portsmouth dockyard. He happened to have his telescope trained on the spire when, suddenly, it folded up "like a concertina", and disappeared. His surprise may readily be imagined.

These earlier troubles contributed to the cathedral's present ones, for some of the fire-damaged stones of 1187 were re-used and have resulted in increasing structural weaknesses, whilst in the nineteenth century soft West-of-England sandstone was used by Gilbert Scott for the new spire instead of the earlier Caen limestone. The sandstone looks pleasantly mellow but has little lasting power and is already badly worn.

Having decided that the renovations could be delayed no longer, the Dean and Chapter were then faced with two severe obstacles. One was a shortage of funds, the other a scarcity of stonemasons. There could be no cutback on the continuous programme of building and repair of churches, halls and schools within the diocese and therefore a special appeal to raise an initial £364,000 within ten years was made. This was achieved a year early and in the meantime local boys were trained to carry out the work. These latter have proved so skilful that the cathedral now operates training schemes for masons on behalf of the Government and sends them to work all over the country.

The future of the cathedral is thus secure. A great deal of restoration still has to be done and for some while yet visitors will have to put up with walking over temporary floorboards and negotiating piles of scaffolding. Much money is still needed but the skill and craftsmanship which is evident in the work which has already been done ensure that contributions continue. Although smaller than many of the great European churches, Chichester Cathedral is nevertheless an enormous structure and dominates the town and the surrounding countryside, especially when seen across the flat expanses of the Selsey Peninsula. Appropriately Chichester is linked with Chartres, and the new ring road which encircles it to the south-west is named Avenue de Chartres.

This road cuts a great semi-circle through the Westgate Fields, a large expanse of green which extends right up to the walls of the cathedral close. Presumably this road had to be built. The town has an east-west by-pass but a fair amount of traffic passes through the centre going north-south and the new road does remove some of it from the vicinity of the Market Cross at the heart of the town. It does not do a great deal of harm to the view across the fields, and would do even less if it were not there at all.

Although its Roman origins are so evident and its cathedral so dominant, Chichester does not live in the past. One of its newest undertakings is a theatre festival of international repute, and it continues to be, as it has for well over a thousand years, a commercial and social centre for the surrounding villages, countryside and coastal region.

Until Dr Russell, the Prince Regent, and the London, Brighton and South Coast Railway Company transformed the whole of the Sussex coast, the least settled area was around the Selsey Peninsula, although its ever-changing aspect had little to do with man, being almost entirely the work of nature. We shall see as we progress eastwards that erosion and the movement of river-beds have affected every part of the coastline, but Selsey provides the most dramatic example of these forces. Not only have large areas of land disappeared beneath the waves, but villages and even a cathedral have gone too. Christianity began in Sussex at Selsey with St Wilfrid, who built a monastery there. Later the monastery church was expanded into a cathedral and remained as such until William the Conqueror ordered its replacement by one at Chichester, by then a far more important centre. To this day lumps of Caen-stone are washed up on the shore and are said to be from the old cathedral, the site of which is now more than a mile out to sea.

As one might expect of an area which has seen so much history and change, the Selsey Peninsula abounds in legends. One, common to districts which have been flooded or encroached upon by the sea, is of bells ringing beneath the water. They are said to be those of Bosham Church, which were removed by a Danish raiding party and carried away in their boats. No sooner had they set sail than the weight of the bells took them to the bottom of the water and there they still are, pealing out in sympathy whenever the present ones are rung. Bosham is the source of a legend known to just about every English schoolboy, that of Canute commanding the tide to recede. He could hardly have chosen a less suitable site for the sea is still encroaching 900 years later. Canute, Earl Godwin, and Harold all lived at Bosham and its church is depicted

Bosham

in the Bayeux Tapestry. The Romans knew Bosham and used its harbour, the palace of Fishbourne being less than three miles distant. Today it is a picturesque village at the end of one of the creeks adjoining Chichester Harbour and is a favourite haunt of yachtsmen.

Due south from Bosham lies the peninsula proper and the Witterings. Wittering itself is beneath the sea but East and West Wittering remain. Vespasian landed here on his way to found Chichester, and 400 years later another chapter in the history of Sussex began when the Viking King Aella and his three sons arrived. Their coming is commemorated by the point, Ella Nore. Wittering's own special legend is that wood from a wrecked vessel of the Spanish Armada, the *Cartagena*, was used in the building of a farmhouse, still called Cartagena Farm.

At the far tip of the peninsula is Selsey itself. Recorded by the Venerable Bede in 681 as an island, save for a strip of land the "cast of a sling in width", it is now a small town of 4,000 inhabitants, crowded with holidaymakers in the summer and the principal centre for commerce and shopping for the surrounding villages. Although busy enough, there is a remoteness about it as if it were still an island. The B2145 which links it with Chichester—one is inclined to write mainland—nine miles distant, passes through a flat, often windswept landscape of occasional houses and cottages and one village, Sidlesham. This latter possesses one of the most handsome of the many old

East Wittering beach, with Hayling Island beyond, and the chimneys and tower-blocks of Portsmouth on the horizon

churches of the peninsula, St Mary's, which dates from the thirteenth century. Flintstone is a particularly common building material in Selsey and there are many houses in the town constructed of it, some having thatched roofs.

The B2145 continues through Selsey and on to Selsey Bill, the very edge of Sussex. The road ends abruptly at the sea wall with the water lapping the foundations a few feet below. It is the most southerly point in the county, further south than either Ryde or Cowes in the Isle of Wight. Selsey Bill consists of a shingle beach, a collection of bungalows and houses and a derelict two-storey flat-roofed hotel, long deserted, with faded, peeling yellow paintwork, and broken-down verandas.

Across the headland and on towards Bracklesham Bay and the Witterings is a sprawl of caravans and chalets. It is impossible to imagine that these insubstantial homes can ever add anything to their setting, but what is the alternative? They provide a holiday right beside the sea at a reasonable price, they are ideal for a family with everything small children need (the beach and the sea being a few paces away, safe from traffic), and they create business for the locals. What has happened at Selsey is typical of much of the Sussex coast but unless access to the seaside is to be denied to all but the privileged few, and given the density of population in the south-east, the development of the shoreline in such a manner was surely inevitable.

Four miles up the coast from Selsey is another chalet development, at Pagham, although the meandering, shallow expanses of Pagham Harbour entail a fifteen-mile journey by road. Despite its long history, Old Pagham has been all but obliterated in the twentieth century, chiefly on account of its proximity to Bognor, of which it is now a part but which was once insgnificant in comparison:

Bognor Regis has a funny little pier, which has a bit missing from the end. The end bit has come off, and is marooned on a sandbank about twenty feet away. The cormorants have taken this over. You can often see their dark forms diving in the water.

In the summer Bognor is invaded by tourists and holiday-makers. They sit under brightly coloured umbrellas, listening to Radio One, while their kids drown each other using plastic ducks as weapons. They all crowd together like a flock of lost sheep, yet if you go about half a mile away from the main bit, it is deserted.

Although these people do lots of damage on the beach, and generally spoil everything, they are essential for Bognor's shops. Anyway, what would Boggy Regis be without all its holidaymakers?

So wrote a twelve-year-old resident of the resort, Freya Newbery, in her school magazine, capturing the essence of what is the most truly family resort on the Sussex coast.

Perhaps because it felt the extensive, sandy beach was attraction enough, perhaps because it feared there would be insufficient members of the middle class to occupy them, the town has never got around to providing its promenade with the row of whitewashed hotels which other Sussex resorts regard as obligatory. Consequently the promenade, particularly east of the pier towards Butlin's holiday-camp, is not very prepossessing, seeming to consist mostly of car parks and amusement arcades.

Bognor

171

THIS FOUNTAIN
WAS ERECTED
TO COMMEMORATE
THE DIAMOND JUBILEE
OF
HER MOST GRACIOUS MAJESTY
QUEEN VICTORIA

FOR SALE

THIS FOUNTAIN
RE-ERECTED
APRIL 19

The Steine, Bognor

172

The view inland from the beach west of the pier, particularly towards the Steine, is better. Here are a number of Regency buildings, none of any exceptional merit and hardly any two alike, but combining with gardens which run down the middle of the Steine to make a pleasing prospect. A prominent feature is the fountain, erected in honour of Queen Victoria, which, whilst certainly not handsome, possesses a certain period fascination. Elsewhere in Bognor there can be few towns where there is less evidence of planned growth.

Close to the Steine is the largest of the not very large— by seaside standards—hotels, the Royal Norfolk, where King George V stayed when he came to Bognor to convalesce in 1928. The King was particularly fond of the town and it is because of his patronage that it is entitled to call itself Regis. Bognor's associations with royalty go back beyond 1928 to its not very distant origins. Until the last years of the eighteenth century it was little more than a collection of fishermen's huts, and no buildings from that time remain.

There then appeared on the scene Sir Richard Hotham, a gentleman who had made a great deal of money constructing hats for the nobility in London. He decided that Bognor was just as suitable as Brighton for royalty to disport itself and he set about turning the fishing village into a fashionable resort. He hoped George III might take up residence but the best he could achieve was Princess Charlotte, the King's granddaughter, who spent the summers of 1808 to 1810 in the town. By then Hotham was dead, a disappointed man, having failed to get the name changed from Bognor to Hothampton. The grounds of his house are now a public park and zoo, whilst the house itself, the most imposing piece of architecture in the town, is a college of education.

Like the rest of seaside Sussex, Bognor has suffered its share of watery misfortunes; an inn, a barracks, and a theatre all being washed away during a severe storm at the end of the last century. The theatre had previously been flooded on a number of occasions, once during a performance, when the actors and audience had to be rescued by boat. The present Esplanade Theatre is its successor, still close to the sea but presumably less vulnerable to it. At one time there was a second theatre, on the pier, but this has now succumbed to Bingo.

Immediately beyond Hotham Park and the holiday camp is Felpham, now a suburb of Bognor but once quite separate from it. As a place of consequence it has a much longer history than the town which has swallowed it up, and possesses a church, the oldest parts of which belong to the thirteenth century. William Blake lived and worked in Felpham from 1804 to 1806, and the thatched cottage which he occupied survives, together with a number of old houses, close to the church. For the rest, Felpham is mostly bungalows, a development which began after the

173

First World War and has gone on edging eastwards through Middleton and Elmer and on the best part of the way to Littlehampton. The oldest have been there long enough to look as though they belong, set in their neat gardens behind privet hedges or rows of miniature firs, and in many ways may be said to epitomize what life in Bognor is all about.

Littlehampton is a friendly, unpretentious place, part resort, part harbour, not particularly large but well able to hold its own against its bigger neighbours, Bognor and Worthing. The best approach is by train, whether along the coast past acres of nurseries and greenhouses, or inland through the Downs with fine views of Arundel and the River Arun. Once past the gasworks and the town dump, one has seen the worst Littlehampton has to offer and as one steps out of the shack-like station a powerful whiff of the sea and ships comes gusting around the corner from River Road and the quays and boatyards beyond.

Like Bognor, Littlehampton has a Butlins; in this instance a funfair, housed in a hangar-like building, not very lovely to look at, despite a screen of trees, but full of delights within. Immediately to the east of the funfair and the river, beside which it stands, is the promenade. The beach beyond is chiefly sand, whilst behind is the Green, a wide expanse of somewhat threadbare grass, an unusual feature and reminiscent of certain French resorts, although there is little else in Littlehampton which is not thoroughly English. Any other associations with France are confined to the area around the harbour whence ships have plied across the Channel and beyond for a thousand years.

There is an attractive little museum in River Road occupying a Victorian semi-detached house. It contains many pictures of Littlehampton over the years, more than one of which features a windmill which used to stand on the site of the funfair. The most interesting aspect of the museum is the building itself, which was at one time owned by a ship's captain. He bought a partially completed sailing ship, laid up in the yard at the end of the road, dismantled it and used its timbers to extend the house; they are clearly visible, portholes and all, at the rear.

For a good many years ocean-going sailing-ships were built at Littlehampton and, whilst those days are over, the yards are busier than ever with the construction of yachts and motor-cruisers. Coasters and timber-ships keep the port busy, necessitating a swing-bridge which until recently carried all the traffic entering or leaving the town from the west. This could handle only a single file at a time, entailing a good deal of congestion, but recently a fixed bridge has replaced it upstream from the quays and the old bridge is now solely for the use of pedestrians.

The river effectively prevents any expansion of the town to the west. The High Street, the principal shops and

Littlehampton

the funfair are all within a stone's throw of the river, but once beyond the boat-yards there is open country. Much of this consists of a golf-course extending southwards to sand-dunes. A small ferry, propelled by an outboard motor, links the east and west banks, close to the club-house, and does considerable business carrying boat-owners across the harbour to their moorings on the west bank.

Stormy seas at Rustington

176

In Roman times, Hampton—its original name—was a good mile back from the sea and it only became a port of any significance and acquired its prefix in the seventeenth century when erosion effectively closed Arundel to sea-going vessels. There are a few oldish pubs and quayside buildings on the east bank but otherwise the town is solidly Victorian, the boarding-houses being situated in quiet roads behind and beyond the Green.

As at Bognor, the nineteenth- and twentieth-centuries spread of the town has swallowed up at least one village, in this case Rustington. It has an old church with a thirteenth-century chancel, but otherwise is chiefly notable for marking the western limit of an almost continuous rash of bungalows, extending along the coast upwards of ten miles as far as Hove.

Rustington leads on to a succession of former villages, each ending in 'ing' (Saxon for 'place of'); Ferring, Goring, Durrington and Worthing. Although a limited number of the bungalows and houses along the coast between Littlehampton and Worthing are for the use of holidaymakers, the majority are permanent homes. Consequently there is nothing of the air of a shanty-town about them; quite the opposite, many of the houses, in private roads, being palatial. Because so many of them are owned by retired people, the gardens at any time of the year are most carefully tended, and in high summer there can be fewer places in England sporting such a

Worthing

concentration of lovingly nurtured and precisely calculated colour.

It may be that this section of the coast was a pleasanter spot, in a quiet sort of way, before the coming of the speculative builder, but time and care have smoothed away the harsher crudities and created neatness and order, not thrilling virtues, perhaps, but not negligible ones either.

Many's the time that I have dwelt
at Worthing, and whilst there, have felt
Some mystery about the place—
Some secret triumph in the face
of everyone I met, as though
Only at Worthing could we know
Seaside perfection on the shore
Of England.—And in vain once more
I gazed around; the Esplanade,
the sands on which the children played;
The pier; the bathers in full view—
The sea; the bandstand nice and new;
Baffled again!—But close at hand
A stern policeman chanced to stand.
"Tell me," I asked, "what magic strong
Fills Worthing town the whole year long?"
He raised his head with simple pride;
"We are not Bognor!" he replied.

That poem by Edith C. M. Boodle, published in the

Sussex County Magazine forty years ago, captures perfectly the essence of Worthing. The hero of *The Importance of Being Earnest* could hardly have been called Jack Bognor, but Jack Worthing is entirely fitting. There is sand on the beach, but only at low tide, and whilst day-trippers do go to Worthing the town makes no great effort on their behalf. As it says of itself "It manages to retain the hall-mark of restful charm and dignified atmosphere".

On a coastline unusually favoured by the elderly and invalid, Worthing stands supreme, and over one third of its population consists of old-age pensioners. There are no hills in Worthing and whilst this results in a town, which in any case is architecturally undistinguished, being visually far less exciting than Brighton or even Eastbourne, it is a great advantage to the elderly. As for the weather, Worthing claims that the mildness of its winters is "probably unequalled on the English mainland". It can point to an average of 553 hours of sunshine each winter for the last thirty-five years, a record; and it needs something out of the ordinary to bring snow to the town, regardless of the severity of conditions up on the Downs or in the surrounding countryside.

Worthing, inevitably, began as a small fishing village, its only distinction being a long-standing charter to hold a market. In 1797 Princess Amelia, the sister of the Prince Regent, visited it, having heard of its mild climate. She extolled its virtues to her relations and thence forward it

The front, Worthing

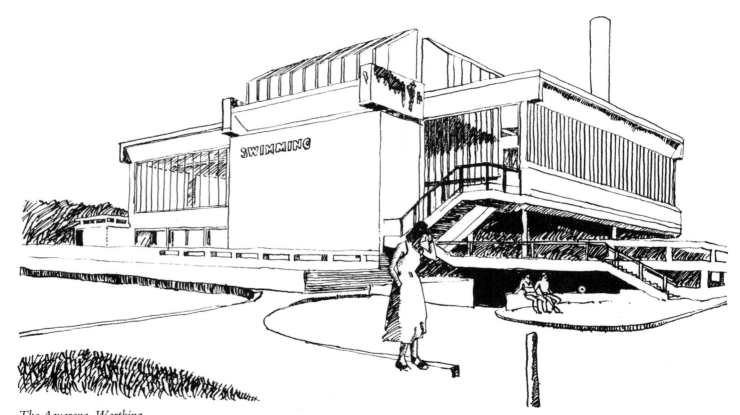

SWIMMING

The Aquarena, Worthing

180

was favoured by royalty, two queens (Caroline and Adelaide) in particular spending much time in the town. The pattern familiar elsewhere on the Sussex coast was repeated, royal patronage ensuring the town's transformation, and it at once began to grow. It expanded both inland and to the east and west, swallowing up the surrounding villages, and extending right up to the Neolithic camp of Cissbury on the Downs. It was incorporated in 1890 and is now, after Brighton, the largest town in Sussex.

The most fashionable end is the west, the majority of hotels being on that side of the pier, along the Marine and West Parades. The older, smaller ones lie to the east, past the South African war memorial and the Steyne, towards Splash Point, so-named on account of the spray which breaks over it when seas are rough. In all, the front extends for $4\frac{3}{4}$ miles. Before Worthing became a resort a large expanse of grass extended along the front—as still exists at Littlehampton—but erosion has turned this to sand and shingle.

Worthing has sixty-one churches and other places of worship, and two cinemas, twenty-one lines in its guidebook devoted to orchestral concerts and four to discotheques. At three o'clock on most afternoons throughout the year the Worthing Municipal Orchestra swings sedately into the light classics at the Pavilion, and on Sunday evenings in summer it accompanies guest artistes in celebrity concerts. The Assembly Hall, part of the Town Hall, is the home of two full-sized orchestras; the Worthing Symphony, and the Worthing Citizens. The Worthing Concert Orchestra also performs there, as does the Municipal Choir and visiting BBC orchestras. Musicals are put on at the Pavilion and the Connaught Theatre. Worthing is a great place for amateur dramatics, the standard of the best of them being virtually professional, which keeps the resident repertory company at the Connaught on its toes.

The proximity of Brighton inevitably means that a good many of Worthing's young people look to it for entertainment, but Worthing makes considerable efforts in providing sporting facilities. The World Bowls Championships have been held in the West Park Sports Centre at Durrington, a complex which caters for many indoor and outdoor activities, whilst national swimming championships take place on occasion at the handsome Aquarena, built by the promenade in 1968.

The pier dates from 1862, although its super-structure is more recent, having suffered, like most Sussex piers, from the ravages of the sea. It was bought by the Corporation, for £19,000, at the end of the First World War. The Pavilion at the shore end was rebuilt in the early 1920s but nevertheless manages to look pure Edwardian; there are two further pavilions, one an amusement arcade, the other a café, bar, sun-lounge and home of a model railway. A stroll along Worthing Pier is a condensed journey through the history of twentieth-century seaside architecture; past the French Empire Edwardiana at the north end, along wooden decking with the glazed windbreak running down the middle, beyond the small centre pavilion and its 1930s curved glass in the manner of Bexhill's famous De la Warr Pavilion, to the contemporary chiefly glass construction at the sea end.

The road from Worthing to Shoreham is one of the dullest bits of the coastline, apart from some crazy architectural forays here and there, and the memory of a film studio which for a time produced epics which rivalled those of Hollywood in popularity, until it was destroyed by a fire in the 1920s. Northwards there are views to Lancing College, a marvellous example of the Gothic Revival, standing against the Downs and one of the best-known landmarks in the county. Shoreham Airport, between Lancing and the coast road, or to give it its full title, Brighton, Hove and Worthing Municipal Airport, is the only commercial one in the county, apart from Gatwick. Its origins go back to the early days of flying but its position—between the railway, the road, the Adur and residential development—has restricted its growth and it is used exclusively by light aircraft.

Shoreham is unique amongst Sussex ports in that it has maintained its importance for a thousand years and more. It may well have been existence in Roman times and was considered by the Normans to be a great prize, being bestowed by King William upon the de Braose family. It was they who built the churches in Old and New Shoreham; St Mary de Haura, in the latter, being particularly fine. It has a Norman tower and transepts, but its great glory is its Early English chancel with a vaulted roof, supported by flying buttresses. There is the odd fragment of ancient building and flint wall elsewhere, mostly in the High Street, but it is all insignificant in comparison with later developments.

The River Adur emerges into the sea at Shoreham and like all Sussex rivers it has changed its course from time to time; these changes have affected the town but have left its importance unimpaired. Shoreham was at one time the principal port for Normandy; King John landed here when he returned to claim the English throne after the death of his brother Richard; and Charles II escaped from it after the Battle of Worcester. A much more recent royal visit was by the Duke of Edinburgh in 1958 when he opened the lock which bears his name.

The extent of the modern port is easily seen, for it runs parallel to the coast road, eastwards from the High Street, through Southwick and Portslade, until it becomes Kingsway, across the border between West and East Sussex and into Hove. Originally this eastern extension was part of the river but it is now a canal, the Adur entering the sea at Kingston-on-Sea by what is known as the

Shoreham

Colliers unloading at Portslade

Western Arm. At low tide there is only four feet of water and the river passing beneath the long bridge which carries the coast road into the town is a mere trickle, with the boats marooned on the mud.

In order to ensure that the much larger ships which berth at the eastern arm have sufficient water, a series of lock gates have been installed and quite big oil tankers and colliers pass through them to reach Portslade Power Station. Shoreham also carries on a considerable trade in corn and timber. On the western bank of the estuary are a number of houseboats some of them very odd-looking contrivances, converted from a variety of one-time sea-going craft, naval and otherwise. There are always a great many pleasure-craft in and around the harbour, which they share with the fishing fleet; Brighton and Worthing boats are both registered in Shoreham.

The rise of Newhaven in the nineteenth century led to a temporary decline in the fortunes of Shoreham, despite the latter possessing the first railway in Sussex. Passenger boats have long ceased to call at Shoreham, but in other respects the last few years have seen a great revival and, with a water front extending five miles from Old Shoreham to West Hove, it is the largest commercial harbour anywhere on the coast between Southampton and Dover.

The eastern end is an area of heavy industry unique to Sussex; there are large numbers of oil storage tanks, with tankers tied up alongside, whilst across the basin are colliers from the north-east, dwarfed by a massive coal dump behind a high brick wall, all in turn made miniature by the enormous bulk of Portslade Power Station and its towering chimneys, the latter dominating the western skyline of any view from Brighton and the Downs. A sunset seen from the promenade, with the uncompromising simplicity of Portslade's twin towers contrasting with the delicate tracery of Worthing Pier, silhouetted against the

Hove Town Hall

185

glowing orange western sky, is a spectacle of nature assisted by man, not easily forgotten.

Hove and Brighton are officially two separate towns, but so inextricably are their histories and present-day development linked that they can hardly be dealt with separately. Therefore the story of Hove will chiefly be found in the chapter dealing with Brighton. A number of features usually considered part of the Brighton scene— the Sussex County Cricket Club ground, Brunswick Terrace, St Ann's Well Gardens where Dr Russell discovered the Chalybeate Spring—are actually in Hove, and it is impossible to tell where one ends and the other begins unless one consults a map.

Yet Hove possesses a character of its own. It is essentially a dignified place, full of handsome, nineteenth-century terraces and squares, much sought after as a residential and retirement area, and sufficiently far away from the noisier jollifications which break out in Brighton from time to time to ensure peace and quiet.

Although not incorporated until 1898, Hove decided sometime before this that it was not to be outdone by other Sussex resorts and it commissioned the celebrated Victorian architect Alfred Waterhouse, creator of the Natural History Museum in South Kensington and of Manchester Town Hall, to produce suitable municipal offices. Hove Town Hall was opened in December 1882, with the sort of beanfeast considered essential on such occasions, the only damper being the non-appearance of the expected Prince of Wales; the bells continued, however, to peal "God Bless the Prince of Wales".

Waterhouse's town hall was grandly impressive, built of red brick and terracotta, and on 9th January 1966 it went out in a fittingly florid manner, being gutted in the largest fire Hove has ever seen. Now a fine Civic Centre stands in its place. Designed by John Wells-Thorpe, it has cost nearly £2 million. Built chiefly of reinforced concrete and glass, its centre piece is the Great Hall. Sufficiently well illuminated by glazed roof-lights to make artificial lighting unnecessary during the daytime, it can accommodate 1,400 people, and is used for all sorts of functions from banquets to wrestling matches. Surrounded (apart from a matching multi-storey car park opposite) on all sides by Victoriana, it reflects great credit on normally conservative Hove, and is much more distinguished than a lot of the half-hearted modernism down the road in Brighton.

CHAPTER TEN

Brighton

Brighton has something for everyone. In the sheer numbers of visitors it attracts it outstrips all other Sussex resorts and it is certainly the equal of any elsewhere around the shores of Great Britain. Take away the seaside and its rivals would be much less, but if the English Channel suddenly quit the front at Brighton there would remain a town of unique interest. For a great many people who live and work in Brighton the presence of the sea at the south end of the town, whilst hardly to be ignored, is of no greater relevance than the Tower of London is to most of the citizens of Tower Hamlets.

It all began in 1750. In that year Dr Richard Russell, a native of Lewes, published *A Dissertation Concerning the Use of Sea-Water in Diseases of the Glands*. This hardly sensational sounding work had a remarkable effect upon the small fishing town of Brighthelmston. The essence of Dr Russell's thesis was that salt-water possessed powerful healing properties. This fact had been known to the medical profession for a very long time, but it happened that the appearance of Russell's book coincided with an upsurge of interest in such matters amongst the general public. The result was the English seaside resort.

It was recommended that one not only bathed in salt water but drank it too, although only if one had a strong stomach; and the Chalybeate Spring, which is now in St Ann's Well Gardens, Hove, immediately became popular. But it was the sea-bathing which really brought the nobility and aspiring nobility to Brighton. Royalty, in the shape of the younger brother of George III, first appeared in 1765. The other brothers followed suit and then in 1783 there arrived the King's eldest son, the Prince Regent. He, more than anyone else, subsequent to Dr Russell, was responsible for the transformation of Brighton. Russell himself died in 1759, five years after settling in the town in what was then its biggest house on a site now occupied by the Royal Albion Hotel.

Having completed the prologue of the story of modern Brighton, let us look at the Brighthelmston which preceded it. The first known inhabitants of the site were Neolithic men, who had a camp up in the Downs just south of the present racecourse. At the time of the *Domesday Book* three manors occupied the area, the chief business of the inhabitants being fishing. They lived mostly beneath the cliffs, in a setting rather like the old part of Hastings, but the sea was encroaching upon them all the time, and in the fourteenth century a new town was begun further inland. East, West and North Streets are reminders of this; South Street having long since disappeared beneath the sea. Severe storms in the first decade of the eighteenth century wiped out all that remained of the old town, the fishermen having in the meantime transferred their homes to the south end of the new town. Immediately to the east was the Steine, a word of Scandinavian origin which originally meant 'stone' but had come to be used as the name for an open space. On it the fishermen laid out their nets to dry, beside a stream which rose in the Downs at Patcham and ran down through Pool Valley into the sea.

With the transformation of the town, at which time its name became shortened to Brighton, much of the old fishing port disappeared and the fishermen themselves were given short shift. Despite their protests the Steine was fenced in and became a garden around which the gentry promenaded. Many found more lucrative employment catering for the latter's needs, some retaining their links with the sea by becoming dippers. Being a dipper must have been a rather satisfying occupation for it consisted of seizing the scruff of a noble neck as its owner emerged from a bathing machine, dragging it into the water and plunging it under for as many times as its owner could stomach such robust treatment. Fishing, although no longer playing a key role in the economy of the town, never entirely disappeared, and at present some 100 fishermen are still resident, although there is said to be only one for whom it is a full-time occupation.

The area around the Steine was one of the earliest parts of the new Brighton to be built up and one or two of the houses on the east side retain their original façades, dating from the nineteenth century. On the west stands the Royal Pavilion, perhaps the most celebrated piece of seaside architecture in the country and one which has received volumes of both abuse and praise, according to the fashions of the times. Nash is usually credited with its design but in reality practically everyone from Mahomed to Mrs Fitzherbert can claim to have had a hand in it.

The Pavilion started out as a perfectly ordinary farmhouse belonging to the Kemp family—the lords of the manor—which the Prince Regent leased for Mrs Fitzherbert in 1786, and it was then the fun started. Henry Holland was commissioned to convert it into a marine pavilion, which he did by enlarging it and adding a rotunda, amongst other things. Then came a riding house and stables, covered by a large dome, and finally in the year of Waterloo, Nash was let loose upon it. Nothing designed by that very classical architect up until then bore much relation to the appearance of the Pavilion on its completion in 1822 and there can be no doubt that it was principally the Prince Regent's baby. The fantastic and unfamiliar shapes then being encountered in India by Wellesley's army as it continued the British conquest there were

The Royal Pavilion, Brighton

189

enjoying something of a vogue in architectural circles and the Prince decided that some "Hindoo" domes, pinnacles and columns would be just the thing for Brighton. In fact the style was more along the lines of a Mahomedan mosque but at that distance from its source of inspiration what was in a name?

With an exuberance and disregard of logic typical of the later Regency and early Victorian periods the interior is principally Chinese, with lashings of bamboo, dragons, serpents and the like. As was not to be wondered at the Prince Regent, by now King George IV, found it all a bit too much and preferred not to live there. Both William IV and Queen Victoria liked it well enough and Prince Albert enjoyed bathing in the sea, but the annual royal visits ended in 1845, by which time Brighton was far from the exclusive resort of twenty years earlier. It had cost around £1 million to build, and Queen Victoria was quite happy to get shot of it to Brighton Corporation for £50,000. Much of the original furnishings were removed and for years it was neglected. Now, the wheel of fashion having come round again and deposited the Pavilion in a position of some eminence, it has been extensively restored. The present Queen has retrieved some of the furnishings and had them put back and the building which may be said to be the precursor of the entire "seaside architecture" style is as splendid as it ever was. Not surprisingly, its almost comically ornate interiors bring tears of joy to the eyes of film-makers, and they have featured in a variety of roles, the best known of recent years being as a setting for the wooing of Barbra Streisand by Omar Sharif in *Funny Girl*.

The Corporation, on acquiring the Royal Pavilion, put it to a great many uses. In 1859 art classes began in the kitchens (the beginnings of the present college of art) and were moved in 1877 to a purpose-built school in Grand Parade opposite. In Victorian times the study of art was a very regimented business under the strict control of headquarters at South Kensington, later the Royal College of Art, whence all decrees on what was good taste emanated. A succession of reproductions of Greek columns, busts and statues was despatched to Brighton for the students to copy. In the afternoon ladies and gentlemen were catered for, chiefly aspiring drawing masters and governesses for the many families in Brighton and Hove which considered artistic instruction for its younger members essential; whilst in the evening it was the turn of the artisans, shop assistants and the like, their course being more concerned with design.

After the First World War Ronald Horton became principal and under him the college attained a world-wide reputation for teacher-training. In 1967 the out of date and unsuitable building of ninety years earlier was superseded by a new one on the same site and today a place on the B.A. course beside the sea in the traditionally artistically inclined town of Brighton is much sought after by students all over the world.

Whilst the Royal Pavilion was being built and extended large amounts of less exotic but often distinguished architecture were appearing in the town. At the beginning it never occurred to anyone to site his residence actually looking out to sea—fishermen's cottages may have done so but that was an inevitable disadvantage which went with the job—and Dr Russell himself took care to ensure that it was his back door rather than his front which faced the beach. Therefore the Royal Crescent, put up at the turn of the century, was considered a revolutionary development for it afforded its residents an uninterrupted view of the Channel and unlimited opportunity to sample the sea breezes on top of the cliffs on the eastern extremity of the town. Once the precedent had been established developers and builders fell over themselves and between 1820 and 1840 the sea-front at Brighton was built up and extended at a speed and on a scale unique in Great Britain.

Two architects are chiefly associated with this period, Charles Bushby and Amon Wilds. Between them they were responsible for a good part of Kemp Town, which was begun in 1823. The most ambitious feature of this was Lewes Crescent and Sussex Square, a huge estate based on Nash's Regents Park Terraces. In order to ensure complete unity the façades were built first and it was many years before all construction behind them was complete, the last

The Kemp Town end of the Promenade, Brighton

residence not being occupied until the 1850s, twenty years after the deaths of the architects, who died within six days of each other in 1833. At the other end of the promenade, in Hove, their chief work was Brunswick Square and Terrace, a project known at the time as Brunswick Town, such was its extent.

191

*Brunswick Terrace and Kingsway,
linking Hove and Brighton*

Keeping pace with all this was the development of the front itself. As late as 1826 Constable's paintings of Brighton show a beach with fishing-boats berthed on it extending right up to the houses. But the fashionable demanded a proper roadway upon which they might drive their carriages and promenade, and a long stretch extending from Brunswick Terrace westwards through Hove was opened by George IV in 1822 and named Kingsway. A sea-wall to protect the centre of the town came three years later and gradually the whole of the front, some four miles in all, was enclosed.

It might be thought that so many grand and imposing buildings, all of a period, would have moulded the character of Brighton for all time. If they had then it would be a seaside Bath or Harrogate, but Brighton has never been the sort of place to bother overmuch with introspective self-definition and no sooner had it established a reputation as the most elegant and refined of seaside towns than the railway arrived and quite transformed it again.

The town's growing importance had encouraged stage-coach proprietors to work wonders with schedules and the eight hours which had been considered almost breathtaking for the fifty-three-mile journey between London and Brighton in the first decade of the nineteenth century had come down to just over $3\frac{1}{2}$ hours twenty years later. This latter was astonishingly fast and was made possible by macadamized roads and the changing of horses every ten miles. Even today this is no more than is asked of the cars in the annual Old Crocks Veteran Car Run. No less than fifty-two coaches were working the route in 1815, the single fair being six shillings. In 1973 British Rail would take one from East Croydon to anywhere on the Sussex coast and back for fifty pence.

The railway reached Brighton in 1841. However intensive the stage-coach service it was as nothing compared with what was now possible. Whereas previously only the middle and upper classes ever visited the sea, apart from those working people who happened to live within walking distance of it, now anyone could go. Brighton was both the first and the nearest seaside town to be connected by rail with London and the ordinary people flocked to it. Its popularity has never waned and today something like seven million visitors come each summer.

The court visits had always run from the autumn through the winter into early spring, but the ordinary holidaymaker naturally preferred to come in the summer. Thus Brighton now had an all the year round season, and although the court soon departed the town got used to doing business for the whole twelve months. This tradition has remained and the front at Brighton in winter seldom has the deserted air common to other resorts.

The very first railway in Brighton was not that connecting it with the capital but a much smaller one, to the port of Shoreham, which was opened in 1840. For the London

Brighton Station

194

opening in September 1841, a magnificent terminus, built on a curve, and designed by Mocatta, was put up at the north end of the town, hard against a chalk cliff. As I write the great arches look especially magnificent, freshly painted in two shades of magenta, picked out in gold, but sadly they are threatened by demolition and replacement by office development. The Victorians delighted in their new form of travel and built palaces to provide a fit means of beginning and ending a journey. The railway still being the most civilized means of getting about quickly and safely, one wonders why our attitude should be any different. Strenuous efforts are being made to save Brighton Station and one hopes they may succeed.

On the slopes below the station and up the further ones on the far side of London Road, working class Brighton took root. Row upon row of two-up and two-down terraced cottages sprang up along the steeply inclined streets, and but for the absence of the mills and their smoking chimneys a holidaymaker from Bolton or Rochdale might have thought himself back home. Industry did come to Brighton, the railway being the chief one, and there were many others, perhaps the most famous being Tamplin's Kemp Town brewery, extensively advertised in later years on the towns trams, trolleys and buses. But for most working people catering for other's enjoyment was their likeliest occupation. In the wake of the grand terraces of the Regency and early Victorian eras came the huge, florid hotels of the second half of the nineteenth century, erected to cater for the newly rich industrialists from the North and the Midlands.

The lot of the working people of Brighton in those days was a grim one. In 1842 one fifth of all deaths in Brighton was caused by consumption, a higher proportion than even Liverpool could claim, then generally regarded as the unhealthiest town in the United Kingdom. There were 86 smallpox deaths in 1841, 130 scarlet fever ones the following year. Around Edward Street, a steep thoroughfare leading from the Steine to Kemp Town, there were courts with open cesspools which were often overflowing. The smell was foul and was not improved by the presence of a number of slaughterhouses in the vicinity. The drainage was primitive, the water supply meagre, although some houses were so damp that lichen grew on the walls and water streamed down them. Dr N. P. Blaker, the consulting surgeon of Sussex County Hospital, wrote a book drawing attention to the plight of the working class, and noted that some of the worst houses were lived in by fishermen. At the same time he remarked that fishermen's families tended to be healthier than many others and supposed this was because they had access to fresh fish and that they got "plenty of fresh air through cracks and crevices", in the walls and floors of their homes.

The poor tried to alleviate their miseries by drinking

and on Edward Street the policemen deemed it wise to walk around in pairs. A large new sewer which emptied into the sea above Rottingdean was completed in 1874 and heralded a general improvement in the health of the town although the process was a slow one; even today Sussex pumps five times the national average of sewage into the sea. But perhaps we should not dwell too long on the miseries which accompanied Brighton's meteoric rate of expansion. There was another side to the story, told to perfection in Arnold Bennett's *Clayhanger*.

Edwin Clayhanger finds himself on the sea-front, Kings Road, having just arrived by Pullman train from the Potteries in a "gilded vehicle" with a "vast interior" which has already removed a large amount of his breath, and he now prepares to expel the rest.

It was vaster than any imagining of it. Edwin had only seen the pleasure cities of the poor and of the middling, such as Blackpool and Llandudno. He had not conceived what wealth would do when it organized itself for the purposes of distraction ... For miles westwards and miles eastwards, against a formidable background of high, yellow and brown architecture, persons the luxuriousness of any one of whom would have drawn remarks in Burslem, walked or drove or rode in thronging multitudes. Edwin could comprehend lolling by the sea in August, but in late October it seemed unnatural, fantastic. The air was full of the trot of glossy horses and the rattle of bits and the roll of swift wheels, and the fall of elegant soles on endless clean pavements; it was full of the consciousness of being correct and successful ... And the enormous policemen, respectfully bland, confident in the system which had chosen them and fattened them, gave as it were to the scene an official benediction.

The bricks and stucco which fronted the sea on the long embanked promenade never sank lower than a four-storey boarding-house, and were continually rising to the height of some gilt-lettered hotel, and at intervals rose sheer into the skies—six, eight, ten storeys—, where a hotel, admittedly the grandest on any shore of ocean, sent terra-cotta chimneys to lose themselves amid the pearly clouds. Nearly every building was a lodgement waiting for the rich, and nearly every great bow-window, out of tens of thousands of bow-windows bulging forward in an effort to miss no least glimpse of the full prospect, exhibited the apparatus and the menials of gormandize.

Over the years many of our greatest writers have been attracted to Brighton. Before Bennett there was Dickens. He stayed in the town on a number of occasions over a long period from the late 1830s to the early 1860s, working on *Oliver Twist*, *Barnaby Rudge*, *Bleak House* and *Dombey and Son*. The Bedford Hotel, on the promenade, where he stayed, bears a plaque commemorating the fact, although the present building is not the one Dickens knew, this having been burnt down in recent times. Brighton features particularly in *Dombey and Son* and Chichester House on the corner of Chichester Terrace is said to be the prototype of the school at which Dombey's son is educated. Possibly it is but Dickens's description of it as being "particularly brittle and thin" is somewhat at variance with the solid lump of Victoriana which presents itself today. Jane Austen wrote of the military camp on the Downs by Brighton racecourse, Thackeray set a good deal of *Vanity Fair* in Brighton, Oscar Wilde went to school in the town, Kipling lived at Rottingdean until the crowds drove him to the seclusion of Batemans at Burwash, and the greatest of contemporary writers, Graham Greene, became a household name with *Brighton Rock*.

Almost exclusively set in Brighton, *Brighton Rock* gives a marvellous, if not flattering picture of the town in the 1930s. It is a violent book and at the time Brighton could be a violent place; a salutary reminder that sunny, prosperous Sussex did not entirely escape the consequences of the Depression years. Brighton had slums in plenty and as late as the 1960s there was a sufficiently high proportion of the electorate aware of the inequalities of life to return a Labour M.P.

In 1823 Brighton acquired its first pier. Initially its purpose was to enable passengers to get to and from the steamers, but it also had shops and stalls and a bandstand and facilities for bathers, and it soon became a favoured rendezvous. In effect it was four suspension bridges, hence its name, the Chain Pier. It lasted almost to the end of the

St Bartholomew's, towering above derelict Victorian terraces, Brighton

197

century, being demolished by a storm just before Christmas, 1896, two months after it had been declared unsafe and closed. Pictures of it by Turner and Constable can be seen in the Tate Gallery.

The Chain Pier had two successors, both of which survive, at least for the present. The West Pier, which is almost in Hove, was opened in 1866; the Palace Pier in 1898. The former is aesthetically the more imposing but the latter is the more popular. Both represent to perfection what the seaside is all about.

Insubstantial yet massive, vulgar, elegant fantasies, they, like the Prince Regent's Pavilion, have been derided and praised according to the tastes of the time. The West Pier remains essentially Victorian but the Palace Pier has something of every era through which it has lived. Down-and-outs, students, the homeless, the holidaymaker without lodgings, all have slept and sometimes made love beneath it. On its surface thousands more may lie all day in deck-chairs until their skins are the equal of the red in the illuminated Union Jack suspended above them, they ride the ghost train, learn their fortunes, relive epic Cup struggles with lead footballers in oversize jerseys, spend their pennies on a hundred different slot machines, play bingo, fish, drink tea, cola, beer and spirits, dance, take a ride in a speedboat and walk about.

The Palace Pier extends far enough from the shore for even the tallest buildings on the promenade, giants dwarf-ing Arnold Bennett's Victorian skyscrapers, to look a very long way off, and one may imagine oneself far out at sea, enjoying all the delights of that sensation without any of its possible perils.

Yet even within a few hundred yards of the beach the English Channel is not to be trusted. On the night of Friday 19th October 1973, during a gale a barge was swept against the pier. The wind and the waves repeatedly smashed it on to the iron supports and eventually a number of them on the west side gave way. Part of the pier slid into the sea and more tilted over but held on. It remained in this perilous state for many months, partially closed to the public, until it was repaired.

The West Pier appeared healthy enough at this time but in fact was in even more dire straits. It has been closed for some years and needs many thousands of pounds spent upon it if it is to be restored. A strenuous campaign to save it is in progress and various plans have been put forward for its future use, but until the money is found its fate hangs in the balance. One cannot pretend that its disappearance would significantly reduce the number of visitors to Brighton, but something of its character would be lost. It is no ordinary resort; ordinary resorts make do with one pier, and it is fitting that Brighton should have two. The Palace Pier will no doubt always survive, but how sad it would be if its beautiful companion vanished. Brighton is a wealthy town and although the corporation has been

The West Pier, Brighton

loth to take action it may be that public opinion will eventually force it to.

The present Corporation is a descendant of the sixty-four commissioners set up by Act of Parliament in 1773 to take charge of the rapidly growing town. In 1810 these were increased to 100, the population of the town then being 12,000 having more than doubled in the previous two decades. By 1825 it had doubled again and the commissioners were once more increased, this time to 112. To be eligible for a vote a citizen had to pay at least £20 in tax each year and the wealthier he was the more votes he was entitled to. The same 1825 Act laid down that there should be no more thatched roofs in the town and that no street should be narrower than thirty feet. A year earlier street lighting had been introduced by the Brighton Gas Light and Coke Company.

The Town Hall dates from 1830 but it was not until 1854 that the Corporation, complete with a mayor, was set up. The population had then risen to close on 70,000. Brighton achieved County Borough status in 1888 and by the end of the nineteenth century was sufficiently large to have spawned suburbs. Still it grew, out towards the Downs, beyond Preston Park, and past Kemp Town, and in 1927 officially swallowed up the former villages of Patcham, Ovingdean and Rottingdean.

Sometimes a particular development can be dated by the names of the streets. One such is the district to the east of the Lewes Road, opposite the Preston barracks, where a number of roads, Mafeking, Ladysmith, etc., have Boer War associations. Then there is a Pankhurst Avenue beside the General Hospital, and a section of the ring road, in Hove, is called King George VI Avenue. Elsewhere the logic determining street names is baffling. A number of thoroughfares recall places elsewhere in Sussex, which is fair enough, although anyone turning into Hailsham Avenue, Berwick Road or Arlington Gardens in Saltdean on the assumption that they are heading in the right direction for any of these destinations is sadly misled. One can understand why Kipling's memory should be perpetuated in Rudyard Close and Rudyard Road, Kipling Avenue and Batemans Road at Woodingdean, close to where he lived at Rottingdean, but why on earth should a number of roads adjoining Hove goods yard commemorate assorted Victorian painters, others half a mile away carry a varied selection of English and Italian ones, and two quite separate districts, one by the cemeteries off Lewes Road, the other north of the Kings Esplanade in Hove, be named after various parts of the Isle of Wight?

One of the greatest employers in Brighton was the railway. In 1852 the works of the London, Brighton and South Coast Railway Company turned out its first locomotive, and for over 100 years was kept busy producing a succession of handsome machines. The most colourful were those designed by William Stroudley their livery being a deep shade of yellow ochre, with red, black, white and green trimmings, brass numberplates and copper-capped chimneys. Small, even by the standards of the time, Stroudley's engines were nevertheless remarkably long-lived, and in 1962, when steam had almost vanished from the Southern Region of British Rail, ten of his famous Terrier tank engines were still at work, the oldest by then being close on 100 years old. Four remain active in Sussex today, two on the Kent and East Sussex Railway, two on the Bluebell. Stroudley's Improved Engine Green, the official, tongue-in-cheek title of his yellow paint, looked a trifle garish on the larger and more powerful locomotives of Stroudley's successors, and during the Edwardian era gave way to a dignified umber. An E4 tank engine of 1897, 'Birch Grove', named after the home of Mr Harold Macmillan, is preserved in this livery on the Bluebell Railway.

Brighton-built engines continued to grow larger—the Atlantics of the Edwardian era were still considered powerful enough to remain in charge of the Newhaven Boat Train into the 1950s—and culminated in the revolutionary Bullied Pacifics of the post-World War Two era. Eight hundred and fifty men were employed at the works in 1947 but ten years later the numbers had declined considerably and with the end of steam—and in an area where traditionally unemployment was low—the works were considered redundant and were closed. Their site, beside the station, is now

One of Stroudley's 'Terrier' locomotives, now at work on the Bluebell Railway

a car-park.

The building of carriages and wagons was transferred from Brighton to Lancing in 1912. This works, too has gone, and the only surviving building associated with the construction of railway rolling stock in Brighton is the former Pullman Car Company's works at Preston Park. Many handsome and luxurious vehicles were turned out here over the years; today a small collection of preserved engines is housed here, although not on display, apart from the occasional open day at the station.

The motor-bus began its career in Brighton in the Edwardian era, although there were trams before this, and

Volks Electric Railway, the seafront, Brighton

trolley-buses succeeded the latter in the late 1930s, lasting for some twenty years. Today services in Brighton are worked jointly by the Corporation and the Southdown Company. The latter's green double—and single-deckers have been a familiar sight throughout Sussex for over sixty years and today there are some 800 vehicles in the company's fleet. The works are at Portslade, where complete overhauls and repaintings are carried out, a number of employees there being formerly at the nearby Harrington works where many of the luxurious Southdown coach bodies were built. A considerable item of expenditure at Portslade is the repair of seat upholstery, damaged by vandalism, the upstairs rear seats of double-deckers being particularly susecptible.

Rural bus services seldom make money anywhere in Britain these days and there have been many curtailments in Sussex in the last decade, although those routes in and around Brighton are still heavily used and the summertime open-top bus service along the promenade is as popular as ever.

Older than any bus service is Volk's electric railway, one of the first electric railways in the world. Built by a local man, Magnus Volk, it now belongs to the Corporation, and its original four-wheel cars still run along the edge of the shingle between Blackrock and the Aquarium every summer.

It is remarkable to recall that aeroplanes were once built

in Sussex but the well-known firm of Caffyns, which has works in Brighton and most of the county's towns, had a hand in the construction of a large number of fighter aircraft during the First World War. Founded by an Eastbourne man, Caffyns was better known for its bodywork for Rolls-Royces, which it built until the mid-1930s. Industrial development since the Second World War has been confined to the outskirts of Brighton, chiefly around Patcham and Coldean on the edge of the Downs. Further east are the handsome buildings of Sussex University, at Falmer in the corner of Stanmer Park. This latter, one of Brighton's most precious and little-known assets, has been threatened for sometime with a ring road; but opposition has been great, and with a growing awareness of how precious the Downs and the countryside around Brighton are it may be that the encroachment upon them is at an end. Certainly the expansion of the town has been much slower of late, with a greater concentration on rebuilding the inner areas, and between 1961 and 1971 the population actually declined from 163,000 to 161,000.

In a manner typical of a town which has always cared more about the present and the future than the past, whilst the West Pier decays a grandiose Marina costing many millions of pounds is under construction further along the promenade. It is situated to the east of Blackrock, almost in front of Roedean School, and incorporates blocks of flats and all manner of wonders, apart from 2,500 berths

A 1929 Rolls-Royce, bodywork built by Caffyns at Eastbourne

and 1,000 hard standings for pleasure-boats. As is the way with such undertakings, a number of modifications have been made to the original plan and a great deal more money has been used up than was anticipated. There is considerable opposition to it, particularly from those who feel that the money could be better spent improving the lot of the less well-off in Brighton, for whom much remains to be done, and whether it will prove worthwhile remains to be seen. What is certain is that it will not go away. If not another shovelful of cement were mixed, that which already stands is substantial enough to last many lifetimes. That being so, it is to be hoped that the Marina, when completed, is both visually pleasing and of benefit to all sections of the community.

One of the most ambitious redevelopment projects in the heart of the town extends from the Promenade, between the piers up to Western Road, the principal shopping thoroughfare which, starting out at the Steine as North Street, continues through to Hove. The project involved the demolition of a lot of buildings which were undistinguished and a certain amount which were not. The best part is Churchill Square, a shopping precinct containing a number of the most popular stores in Brighton, but it is a pity that more of the sea cannot be seen from it for the steep rise up from the Promenade would make a splendid vantage point, were it not for the intervening high buildings and the multi-storey car-park which almost entirely block the view.

Immediately to the east of Churchill Square is the original Brightelmston, an area which one may hope no developer would ever be allowed to tinker with, although in 1935 an alderman was quoted in the *Brighton Argus* as follows, "the charm of this part of the town could be retained by demolishing the entire area and rebuilding an exact replica, but allowing more air and light and the inclusion of all modern conveniences".

In the middle of it are the Lanes, a warren of footways, so narrow that the overhanging upper storeys of the buildings almost touch each other. Antique and book shops and boutiques abound and attract almost as many visitors as the Promenade. There is a small section which is very new, in Brighton Square. Cleverly designed to blend in with its surroundings and very different in concept to that of the alderman in 1935, the area is a great contrast to the souvenir shops on the Promenade, wreathed in a pungent but not entirely unattractive smell of boiled sweets, salt air and not very fresh fish, and the less inviting Queen's Road, the somewhat shabby thoroughfare leading from the sea to the station.

But contrast has always been what Brighton is about and is at the root of its continuing attraction. It has had its moments of violence and misguided spirits have abused its tolerance, but on the whole Brighton does not mind how its residents and its visitors amuse themselves as long as they do not set out to offend others. As a consequence, as I have tried to show, it is unique. It is London-by-the-sea; the mecca of the day-tripper; a source of endless wonder for the sociologist, the students of architecture and rude postcards, the artist and the historian; home for many famous actors; the inspiration of the novelist; in short, a place of almost limitless variety.

Index